Shared Lives

Shared Lives

Building Relationships and Community with People who have Intellectual Disabilities

Roy McConkey

John Dunne

Nick Blitz

SENSE PUBLISHERS
ROTTERDAM/BOSTON/TAIPEI

A C.I.P. record for this book is available from the Library of Congress.

ISBN 978-90-8790-940-6 (paperback)
ISBN 978-90-8790-941-3 (hardback)
ISBN 978-90-8790-942-0 (e-book)

Published by: Sense Publishers,
P.O. Box 21858, 3001 AW
Rotterdam, The Netherlands
http://www.sensepublishers.com

Printed on acid-free paper

TABLE OF CONTENTS

AUTHORS

Roy McConkey

Roy is Professor of Learning Disability at the University of Ulster; a post jointly funded by the Northern Ireland Health and Social Care Board. A psychologist by training and a native of Belfast, he has previously held posts at the University of Manchester, in Dublin and in Scotland. He has authored, co-authored and edited numerous books and research papers in learned journals. He has acted as a consultant to various international agencies and this work has taken him to some 20 countries in Africa, Asia and South America. He is a Fellow of the International Association for the Scientific Study of Intellectual Disability.

John Dunne

John is recently retired as Director of Psychology with the Brothers of Charity Services, Galway, Ireland. He trained as a clinical psychologist in Ireland and the USA, and is an Associate Fellow of the Psychological Society of Ireland. He has had a particular interest in the development of a relationship and community model of service and in the application of positive psychology to the lives of people with an intellectual disability. He is author or co-author of a number of publications, book chapters and articles.

Nick Blitz

Nick is Medical Adviser to the Camphill communities of Ireland; having lived and worked in life-sharing communities for much of his life. Previously, he worked as a research scientist at Imperial College, London and McGill University in Quebec, where he was awarded his PhD on a Commonwealth scholarship. Following a career change, he worked as GP and Medical Officer to the Camphill Schools in Aberdeen and as Medical Consultant to the Camphill Communities in Scotland, before taking up his current post in 1998. He is involved in disability research, and lectures on Camphill courses in disability in Ireland and the UK.

ACKNOWLEDGEMENTS

Our thanks to Ikuka Chiba for the cover photograph; to Special Olympics Ireland for the photograph on page 7; to Colm Lydon for the photographs on pages 57 and 115; and to the Camphill Photo Archive for all others used in the book.

Down through the years we have gained greatly from the many people with an intellectual disability that we have known and from the colleagues with whom we have worked. A particular thanks to Camphill Communities of Ireland, Brothers of Charity Services, Galway and the University of Ulster who facilitated the writing of the book.

TIMOTHY P. SHRIVER, PH.D

CHAIRMAN AND CEO, SPECIAL OLYMPICS INC.

FOREWORD

Shared Lives is a challenging guidebook for how we think about and organize 'support services' for people with intellectual disabilities. But it is far more than that. It is a groundbreaking exploration of the issues of absolute value, self-empowerment and potential contributions of people with intellectual disabilities, a population that has historically been denied all these things.

To understand why this is new territory, it's important to remember how far the movement to promote and protect the civil rights of people with intellectual disabilities has come over the last 50 years. After all, it is only in recent years and even then in far too few places around the world, that people with intellectual disabilities have begun to emerge from society's shadows. For years, the world has seen only their disability, their comparative limitations, their perceived weakness.

Such a narrow view has had severe consequences: stigmatization, isolation and often institutionalization that leaves over 200 million of the world's citizens without even the most basic rights and devoid of self-worth and potential.

This focus only on what people with intellectual disabilities were *incapable of* was pervasive. Even service providers, researchers, supporters and others dedicated to the advancement of the rights and abilities of people with intellectual disabilities have had their work and mindset influenced by this perspective. As a result, even today supporters' efforts often deal primarily with issues that address their disability and their limitations (as seen by people without intellectual disability).

Rarely was the focus on the inherent gifts, talents and abilities of this population. But slowly that has begun to change. As Thomas Merton, the social-activist Trappist monk and poet gently reminded us: *"The beginning of love is to let those we love be perfectly themselves, and not to twist them to fit our own image. Otherwise we love only the reflection of ourselves we find in them."*

So too has it been for those who serve people with intellectual disability. As work to support them has evolved and advanced, supporters on all levels have found themselves recognizing the unique gifts of persons with intellectual disability. They have found themselves being changed by those they set out to "help" as they become part of an ever increasing community that recognizes that they are not working *for* people who had been beset by some trauma or hardship, but instead are working *with* people who dramatically enrich the quality of their lives and their relationships.

Shared Lives picks up where this recognition and dramatic shift take place, and it challenges supporters, service organizations and societies to incorporate it in ways that are focused and action oriented. The book promotes an appreciation of the gifts of people with intellectual disabilities, and works toward an understanding of what it is about this population that can bring about transformative change – not only in themselves, but in others.

Consider it essential reading for not only those of us committed to the respect, acceptance and inclusion of people with intellectual disabilities, but for anyone who works to promote the potential and self-determination of all of us!

SHARED LIVES: AN INTRODUCTION

The real voyage of discovery consists not in seeking new landscapes but in having new eyes.

Marcel Proust

This is a book about people sharing their lives together. Even more, it's about supporting one other as we go through life.

It is about people who down through the years have been called by various names – mentally handicapped, learning disabled, intellectually impaired. But to those who know them well, these labels don't much matter. They have discovered that each person has a unique personality. Unless we get to know the man or woman behind the label as individuals with feelings, talents and aspirations, it will be hard to provide them with the support they need. Nor will we gain from the positive benefits that they can bring to our lives. We need to reduce the divide between 'them' and 'us'.

The book is also about other people who are also given various labels – 'family', 'volunteers', 'staff' or 'professionals'. We all share a common ambition. We want to make life better for the people we are supporting. In many ways, what we do is not remarkable. Some would call it ordinary, even mundane. But what is exceptional, is our persistent willingness to challenge expectations. For example we are prepared to question beliefs about people's supposed incompetence. We try to find ways of supporting them to do things for themselves.

Equally people with intellectual disabilities can enrich the lives of their families, friends and supporters. Often this is overlooked, even ignored. Yet their positive influences are vital in creating resilient relationships that are mutually rewarding. These are the building blocks for creating communities of support that can help to revitalise modern society.

Our aims for the book are simple. We want to present people with an intellectual disability in ways that both addresses their needs and highlights their gifts, in keeping with the thinking of positive psychology[1]. We want supporters to appreciate and reflect on the relationships they have with those they support, since mutual relationships are a primary means of ensuring each other's happiness and enabling each other's development – social, emotional and spiritual. Supporters tend to focus on daily tasks and the role they are expected to fulfil, without realising sufficiently that their work will be all the more effective and rewarding if founded on personal relationships. Finally, we want to explore how people can find the sense of community that can be lacking in urban societies especially.

THE POWER OF STORIES

The book is based around stories from everyday life as they usually illustrate the power of relationships. Many a story is based around adventure, romance and mystery but often we can identify most easily with the stories of ordinary life; as seen in the popularity of television soap operas. Yet their stories rarely feature people with a disability. Why? Maybe it's because these people are perceived to be so different that they can't be part of our everyday lives. Instead they are confined to special settings. Fortunately we are living at a time when society is more aware of discrimination and people with a disability are asking for more than pity or sympathy. Much more can be done to include everyone in community life.

Our stories point to how relationships can come about. They are not prescriptions but rather illustrations of what has happened in people's lives. People change people. Stories can touch us emotionally and it's feelings that drive us to act. It is when support is driven by deep feelings that it changes lives and makes a real difference to the whole person.

WHAT'S IN A NAME?

We had one problem in putting the book together. How do we refer to the people whose stories we tell? People in need of support are not all the same; just as people who are supporters are very different from one another. We decided to use the term '**supporters**' for people who are in a helping role outside of the family.

Supporters are often staff paid to work in a variety of services. They may support people in some form of accommodation or in the person's own home. Or they might work in schools, colleges and day centres or in some form of community-located activity such as employment and leisure schemes. They could be employed to work with only one person or they may support groups of people. In some organisations these roles are fulfilled by volunteers.

But supporters also include people in the community who may volunteer to support people in particular ways; such as friends and acquaintances, leaders in sports and social clubs, co-workers in businesses and so on.

Although the term supporters can include family members – parents, brothers and sisters –in this instance the word 'family' is enough to express the supportive relationships that they nearly always offer to their kin. A major theme of the book is the need to build communities of supporters from these three groupings – paid supporters, community supporters and family.

It was harder to find words for people who need or receive support. Scores of names have been used down through the years and dozens are in daily use in society. The problem with many of these names is that they devalue the persons labelled by them. Who wants to be called 'mental', 'slow' or even 'special'; or known as a 'client' or 'service-user'? In the end we opted for the phrase 'people we support'. More often we shorten it to the word 'people' as a reminder that they are people first. We have more in common with one another than that which separates us. But the full phrase is needed at times to avoid confusion. Although all of us require the support of others, some people need more *life-long* support even in their adult years. This is the group we mainly focus on.

We realise too that grouping people under a common label runs the risk of creating stereotypes when the reality is that people vary a great deal. Our stories are examples of what has happened for certain people in certain places at certain times. You have to take from them the lessons you feel are applicable to you and the people you work alongside.

We are not implying that every story has a happy ending. Supporting people is not easy or straightforward. But appreciating the good times can see us through the challenging and testing periods.

LISTENING WITH UNDERSTANDING

Perhaps the greatest change that has occurred in our thinking about people in need of support in the 21st Century, is a realisation that their voices and views have to be heard and taken seriously[2]. In years gone by, parents and professionals made all the decisions for them with scant consideration as to what they wanted. Such was their vulnerability and powerlessness that they went along with whatever was offered to them. Indeed this can still happen today. But this creates dependency and helplessness that accentuates their disabilities.

Supporting people to live more fulfilled lives means listening to their hopes and fears, understanding their capabilities and needs for support, and helping them to realise their ambitions and cope with the inevitable disappointments. This is no different from what everybody expects from a supportive relationship. But the people we support do not find it easy to speak up for themselves. That's why we must go to extra lengths to ensure we listen to them and to mould our support to their needs and aspirations. We believe that the simple act of listening has the power to transform the relationship between supporters and the people they support[3].

WHAT IS MEANT BY SUPPORT?

The term support is frequently used in modern services. But do we really provide the support that people want and need?

We view support as having four parts as the Figure shows. These are not separate. Rather they are like the colours of a rainbow. These merge into one another and together they produce what we call 'support'. Various chapters of the book are devoted to each strand.

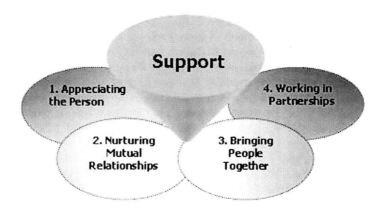

Supporters have to appreciate the personal qualities of the people they support; seeing them as valued citizens who can enrich the lives of their family, their community and their supporters. This entails changing mind-sets to a positive view of people, coupled with greater emphasis on the emotional aspects of the support we provide for them. Equally, the focus has to be on the individual needs of those we support. We must respond to them as persons and not to their labels.

This means getting to know them very well through watching and listening. Chapters 1 and 2 focus on these themes.

In Chapter 3 we describe the features of a supportive relationship and what distinguishes it from other types of relationships. Then in Chapter 4 we examine people's need for mutual relationships and how this can be fulfilled. The supporter's role in helping people to nurture friendships with others is addressed in Chapter 5.

In Chapters 6 and 7 we look at how people and supporters can come together with others in various social networks or communities. These provide a sense of togetherness and belonging while widening opportunities for people to live more active and fulfilled lives through leisure, education and employment.

Chapter 8 examines the building of alliances and the creation of partnership working across different support agencies, organisations and families. There are many obstacles to doing this but for us a starting point is for all agencies to be open to the new opportunities and choices within their localities. This is especially so when it comes to balancing risks with opportunities as we discuss in Chapter 9.

Finally Chapter 10 summarises how all these themes contribute to a sense of personal fulfilment.

THE ESSENCE OF SUPPORT

When these four strands come together, a radically different form of support service emerges. The bedrock is the relationship between two people; the person in need of support and his or her supporter. It is built around individuals – their talents and aspirations – and thrives on people's creativity. It means building supports from the bottom-up. This simple truism echoes throughout these pages. Our primary theme is the power for change that is available in the working and personal lives of individual supporters. The practical steps they can take may seem small on their own, but when added together can greatly enhance the lives of the people we support. A fair number of supporters intuitively support people in these ways without realising the significance of what they do. By naming and describing their contribution, we want to affirm them while also giving other supporters an opportunity to learn from their example.

Given the infinite variety of human nature, we cannot present you with ready-made courses of actions to follow. And in any case, there is often no 'right way' of achieving the outcomes that you desire. Rather supporters have to make the best decisions based on what they know and the circumstances that they are faced with. As we will discover, certain decisions can create dilemmas that are not easily resolved, for example how to balance potential risks with valued opportunities. Supporters need to become adept at analysing and reflecting on the decisions they are called on to make. The final chapter addresses these issues.

RE-FOCUSSING SERVICES

It is increasingly evident that existing service systems can inhibit rather than encourage innovative practices by supporters. Modern health and social service organisations can easily become pre-occupied with paper-work, policies and procedures, health and safety issues and keeping within budgets, so much so that people's feelings, needs and relationships are devalued. Administrative efficiency and accountability has its place but our hope is to redress the imbalance we perceive that is taking hold in 'professionalised' support services. Hence a secondary theme of the book is the new ways of thinking and working that are required to nurture supportive relationships in services and in society.

In essence then, our focus is on people and more especially on recognising and developing their talents. The history of disability services is rooted in managing and treating people's deficits. Fortunately there are various professionals such as nurses, therapists and social workers who can focus on these particular issues. Their jobs and the techniques they employ are important and have their own literature. This book provides a rather different emphasis.

There is a danger that a focus on remediating people's deficits colours all the supports the person receives. A better starting point is the person – full stop! We may well go on to define their special needs as a step in responding to them but this has to be done within the context of helping them to meet their ordinary needs – those that are common to all of us.

SUPPORTING SUPPORTERS

Supporters experience many pressures in their work and often they are expected to cope on their own. Without support they can become dispirited and disillusioned. Many supporters tell us that what keeps them going is the people they work with and we tend to agree. But that may not be enough. Much of what we say in the book applies equally to the relationships that supporters have with one another. Staff may need to be open to support from families of the people they support or from their allies in the community as well as providing these groups with the support they need.

We know that supporting other people is not always easy. Some people can be difficult to get to know, to like and to work alongside. It can be hard for supporters to pull together. We have no easy solutions to offer. But we believe in the human gains that come even from the times of struggle. It makes life challenging, exciting, frustrating, rewarding, exhausting, hilarious, demanding, tedious, fun and worthwhile. Unless we play our part and make the effort, then no relationships will form. We can't wait for others to make the first move. In nurturing relationships, all our lives will be changed for the better.

THE POWER OF POSITIVE EXPERIENCES

*Actor Pierce Brosnan and medal winner Karl Suppan from Austria
at the World Games of Special Olympics, Dublin.*

There will always be the thrill and fascination of watching the elite perform
wonders of the physical. But Special Olympics, in a way, uses sport to capture
wonders of the human spirit.

The Sunday Independent 29.06.03

Some years back, something extraordinary happened in Ireland, when thousands of
athletes came from all around the world to take part in the World Games of the
Special Olympics. At once they won the admiration, the respect, and indeed the
hearts, of the whole country. The media struggled to capture the experience as it
unfolded day by day. The most hardened journalists became like putty in the hands
of the special Olympians, and wrote moving and deeply reflective pieces about
their experience of the games.

Few events have gripped the public imagination so vividly as this enriching experience shared by the entire nation in an extraordinary outpouring of courage, joy, skills and compassion.

Athletes who are categorized by a society as abnormal because they have learning disabilities, demonstrated again and again that they have far greater abilities than some who see themselves as smarter or more able-bodied.

It was an object lesson in humility for us all, a marvellous example of volunteerism by the citizens of host towns and the many professionals and organizers who gave so unstintingly of their time and expertise throughout the past week and more.

Editorial, The Irish Examiner, 30.06.03

Two aspects of the games were highlighted in particular:

– The impact that the athletes had on communities all around the country, releasing a 'latent goodness' which led thousands to volunteer to open their homes and join in celebrating the event; and,

– The renewed awareness of 'the potentiality of every human being' that came through 'glimpses of inspiring humanity.' The athletes were seen as having offered something of great value to the whole of society.

For two weeks the Irish newspapers were full of extraordinary stories that showed that human spirit at its best as seen not only in what the athletes achieved, but also in how they went about it.

THE QUALITIES OF THE ATHLETES

Three particular qualities of the athletes were noted in various reports. First, was their courage and determination:

And then eyes turned to lane one, where the competitor appears to be stuck at the start. As we later find out, Hazel Zumbado, a slight 15-year-old from Costa Rica is deaf and mute and – out of the pool – confined to a wheelchair. She has the use of her arms but her hands don't work properly. So she can swim, but as we clearly see, only with great difficulty. Yet now, slowly but surely, she is moving forward. Rising to her effort, literally, the crowd above the pool is also getting noisy. They are shouting, screaming, urging her every inch of the way; and her progress is measured in inches, as enormous effort translates into tiny advances through the water.

Suddenly the cheering gives way to a rhythmic handclap as when a 5000 meters runner is chasing a world record. There are now four assistants around her in the water, encouraging, and ready to help if needed. But the swimmer is going to make it without their assistance and with everybody in the packed gallery on his or her feet, applauding, she touches the wall in 1 minute 59.23

seconds. 'It's great, isn't it?' says a woman, who has suddenly appeared alongside you. 'Yea, fantastic,' you mutter, looking down pretending to take notes while blinking your eyes repeatedly. 'And the response from the crowd is wonderful,' the woman adds. 'Irish people have really opened their hearts,' the woman is saying. True, you nod still not able to look up and struggling to shut the door on your heart before it embarrasses you any further.

Frank McNally, The Irish Times 26.6.03

Second, athletes' kindness to one another, at times even foregoing the competition to assist others in need:

Half way around the 10-kilometre road race in the Phoenix Park, 30-year-old Swiss rider, Yann Mercet, suddenly started to slow down. Beside him his rival, Andorran, Jordi Julia, had crashed out and without hesitating, Jann eased off the pedals. He freewheeled while he checked his friend was unhurt.

Only when Jordi had remounted, Yann began racing again. The pair headed towards the line in first and second place. Jordi took Gold while Jann a few yards behind the finish happily settled for the Silver Medal. Had he kept going, he would have undoubtedly have won the top prize.

As the Swiss coach congratulated Yann on his medal, the rider seemed entirely unconcerned that four years of hard training near his home in Neufchatel had ended in Silver, rather than the Gold he won at the last World Games in North Carolina. He shrugged as he told me about the race. Of course he would stop for his friend.

Stephen Dodd, The Sunday Independent, 29.06.03

Third, awe at the effort they displayed when competing.

Gary Durkin (14) from Castlebar was an early participant in the Bean Bag lift. He sat in his wheelchair and gazed at the blue and yellow bags. If the silent urging of the audience could have moved them, they would have soared over Ballsbridge. 'I think he needs a little bit of encouragement,' said the MC, Nicola O'Loone. As the audience cheered, Gary stretched out a hand. Then he pulled it back. The hand went out again and the yellow bag was in the air and into the basket. Had he just climbed Mount Everest and abseiled back down in time for tea, Gary wouldn't have received more applause.

Alison Healy, The Irish Times 26.6.2003

THE HEART OF THE GAMES

Press commentators and the volunteers they interviewed tried to define what it was about the Games that affected them so deeply. Central to the experience was the spontaneity, the courage, the openness and the friendliness of the athletes. Possibly the most frequently used word in the media reports was 'heart.' Not just the great heart shown by the athletes, but everybody's heart.

He learned, as all who shared the tennis feeling learned, that, while feet and hands are important in tennis, in the game of life it's the head and heart that count – especially the heart. There were no losers last week. Love all.

Declan McCormack, The Sunday Independent 29.06.03

It caused people to reflect on what often seems absent in modern society. The taxi driver who spent the week shuttling volunteers and families to and fro summed it up:

You know what all this makes you feel like,' he says, 'Like you're not alone, 'cos that's kind of how you feel in this country these days. It's nice. Hope it lasts. I think it will. Maybe we found what we lost. I dunno.

Key to the success of the Games was that they were organised so as to give people personal contact with individual athletes. This happened particularly through the host programme, where people had one or two athletes to stay in their homes the week before the games. Having been deeply touched by their guests, many hosts followed them to Dublin to support them at the Games, and to share once more in the great feeling of togetherness they had known the previous week in their local community. One woman helped host the Irish Golf Team and then found herself arranging a totally unplanned week at the Games golf competition, though never previously interested in the game. "*Oh I had to come. I just couldn't bear it when they left us.*" she explained. "*It was like I was left with a big hole inside.*"

THE ELEMENTS OF SUCCESS

The impact of participants did not happen by chance. The organisers of the World Games deployed five key tactics that all supporters need to heed.

Promote positive images of people

The Games promoted the talents and personalities of the athletes in a wonderful way. People were given opportunities to prove themselves and had their successes applauded. This not only enhanced their confidence and self-esteem, but also changed other people's perceptions of them. This happened both at the Games and in the local communities where the athletes went to stay.

The media played a major role in promoting positive images[4]. Pictures from the World Games were beamed around the world. It is striking to contrast this coverage with the more usual media images of the people with disabilities. More typically these focus on stories of pity and distress, presenting situations where families are under intolerable pressure due to the lack of adequate supports, or where people are being treated badly in some dehumanising service setting. While such exposés are valuable in generating pressure for change, they also create very negative stereotypes of the people needing support. They do not present 'the triumph of the human spirit' that was repeatedly seen in the Games.

Create positive associations

The Games drew on a wide range of celebrities. Some like Nelson Mandela of South Africa and President Mary McAleese of Ireland spoke at the opening ceremony. Many others – well-known film stars, pop stars and professional athletes – presented medals for the various events. This produced many images of formerly devalued people in the clearly delighted company of those who are most highly valued in this age of celebrity.

Use ordinary settings

The Games took place in the wide range of setting used by everybody for major sporting fixtures, and on the whole, athletes took part in the same sorts of competition. They stayed in ordinary homes or in hotels and guesthouses, rather than in disability centres.

Perhaps this was part of the reason for the success of the volunteer programme. It was easier and more comfortable to offer support in ordinary settings rather than being asked to go into rather alien service settings dominated by professionals. Likewise, the people we support have to be seen in the ordinary settings - in shops, bars and buses; in schools, colleges and businesses; and in socially valued settings such as television programmes, theatres and concerts, if we are to encourage the general public to be more engaged with them.

Have a good time

Fun and celebration were major features of the Games, most of it generated by the spontaneity of the athletes and their obvious love of having a good time! This proved irresistible to everybody else. It also meant that people further lost any sense of stigma as they met and mixed with others in a most enjoyable way. Much more can be done in ordinary life to create occasions of celebration and fun that bring all sorts of people together and create bonds between them.

Expect achievement

The World Games presumed that athletes would succeed not fail. The very act of taking part was an achievement for many. Likewise, the expectation of achievement in everyday life should encourage supporters to have people do more for themselves, be it learning to wash their hands or to use a dish-washer. But just as in the Games, participation in community life for some may require hard work and self-discipline so that people do not let themselves down. This coaching role is a key one for supporters.

The positive mindsets created by the organisers of the Games did not happen by accident; nor were they some sort of contrived strategies. They followed naturally from their belief in the athletes that was based on the experience of many years.

The Irish Games confirmed once more how well founded were these beliefs in changing hearts and minds.

THERE WAS A PRICE

By the end of the World Games, people were both exhilarated and exhausted. A great deal of hard work had gone into the Games, not only in Dublin but all around the world, as athletes and their coaches trained and competed in local and national competitions for months and years. It took a great commitment to sustain that effort over such a long period of time.

And there were the hidden and not so hidden times of crisis at the Games – rows among athletes and organisers; despair and exhaustion when hoped-for success did not happen; supporters at the end of their patience; people making unrealistic demands; people feeling unappreciated – and all the other human difficulties that can arise at a pressured time.

But everyone walking out of the stadium after the closing ceremony would have said it was all worthwhile despite the pain. What was achieved repaid the effort a thousand fold. The Games were a wonderful event, but not in a facile or pretty way. It was too real, too human, for that. The athletes stole the show.

WHAT THE ATHLETES OFFER IS WHO THEY ARE

Throughout all the ceremony and competition, the athletes performed simply as themselves. As one writer noted:

> We like the predictable; the organized social dance where we know what to expect and what is expected of us. All this goes out the window when we are dealing with people with an intellectual disability. They haven't learned hypocrisy and prevarication, double speak and phoney. What you see is what you get. If they like you, you'll know it and if you're boring, well you'll know that too. Initially, that's a bit scary but it grows on you – you might even want to continue living this way, ask the volunteers.
> **Marianne O'Malley, The Irish Times 26.06.03**

This experience of deep and accessible humanity made Irish people feel instantly at home with the athletes, despite the barriers of culture or language. People were allowed to glimpse something of their own deepest identity – the part of themselves that is made for relationships with others – and beyond that, by being brought to a place of shared humanity by the athletes and by experiencing a sense of community with them. For a time, this replaced the loneliness that arises from living in a society that values achievement and possessions more than relationship and community.

Wolf Wolfensberger[5] summed up this thought well in a short but powerful article in 1988, where he listed the positive characteristics of those labelled as 'mentally retarded,' and placed first *"their growth of beautiful 'heart qualities'"* and argued that their resources are more concentrated on relationships. Far from being disabled in terms of their capacity for relationships; he saw this as a particular strength for many.

In the professional literature on people with intellectual disabilities, little reference is made to their positive qualities. On the contrary, most of what is in the research journals only highlights the shadow side of those we support, so much so that it distorts our images of their full humanity. For example, we undertook a survey of all articles published in six intellectual disability journals between 1996 and 2000. This showed that out of a total of 2,789 articles, only 21 focussed on anything positive. That is less than 1%, compared to the 99+% that focussed on negative features.

The people we support certainly can have significant problems and challenges to address, and researching these topics can lead to new forms of intervention. In that sense, the negative focus of professional endeavours can have positive outcomes. But overall, the relentless emphasis on the negative in what is written about the people we support has unwittingly contributed to diminishing them rather than celebrating who they are and what they can offer. It is past time to take a fresh look and to find a new, more balanced vision.

AN EXCEPTIONAL EVENT?

Some might say that those Summer Games were a heightened, short-term experience that swept the country along in a tidal wave of emotion. Indeed the Games slogan was '*Share the feeling.*' Did those weeks give an unrepresentative picture? We suspect not because the same feelings are reported by family members and by service supporters who live and work with people every day. But often these remain private experiences that are not celebrated or even acknowledged. The rest of this chapter explores these experiences in more detail but this leaves unanswered the question – why do we fail to see the contribution that certain people bring to all our lives?

It is an important question, because if the experience of the World Games and those wonderful news reports were to be taken seriously in an ongoing way, the public perceptions of people would be rebalanced. They would be seen as

– People of talents rather than deficits;
– People who can achieve rather than being destined to failure;
– People who are responsible rather than dangerous;
– People who are attractive rather than strange; and,
– People who have a great deal to offer to others rather than just needing to be looked after.

As we argue throughout this book, all these changes in how people are seen, have to come as much from the heart as from the head.

THE POSITIVE EXPERIENCE OF SUPPORTERS

The feelings evoked by the World Games are also experienced by families and supporters. They know how the daily shared experiences with the people they support enhances their own lives. Yet this is rarely acknowledged or promoted. More negative images tend to dominate. Even today it is not uncommon for the parent of a child with a disability to be regarded with pity, while service supporters may be seen as 'wonderful people' because of the kind of work they have chosen to do. The reality of people's experiences is far richer and more complex than that. As well as, and sometimes even because of, the undoubted difficulties they can face day-to-day, both families and supporters have a great deal of positive things to report about those they support and the beneficial impact this has on them.

THE FAMILY EXPERIENCE

For parents, the birth of a child with a disability can be a most painful time of disappointment, anxiety and grief. Not unusually in the early months and years, parents meet a series of professionals all asking about their child's problems, with few taking time to enquire about the good times or the positive contribution their child has brought to their lives. Some professionals may add to parents' fear and turmoil by projecting their own unconscious negative images regarding disability.

The emotional upset of parents is seldom resolved once and for all. It often recurs at various points throughout the child's life, particularly at the milestones that may highlight their child's limitations relative to other children. Feelings of guilt or depression may persist; marital strain and separation can happen. Parents' sense of loneliness and helplessness is not helped by having to fight to get the support services that they feel their son or daughter requires. Yet despite all these and other pressures, many if not most parents continue to adapt to the new family member.

> I was told, I cried, but I realised that we are in this together and I was determined to make the best of it. Then I fell in love with the child....

Parents learn to trust their own hearts and to think anew about the child, in ways very different from the unconscious negative images they may have previously held about what it means to have a disability. A desire to love and protect follows naturally from the sense that this child is "ours." Not surprisingly, the family then starts to experience positives associated with having the child.

Up to recently, researchers used a stress-and-coping model when looking at parents and families of children with a disability. Now the realisation has dawned that these families *"are not just coping, they are thriving and positively benefiting from having a member with a disability – they are better people because of the experience."*[6]

A content analysis of 60 books written by parents of children with various disabilities found that in addition to recounting significant demands and emotional stress, the majority of authors also felt that their lives had increased enrichment and meaning as a result of their experience with their children[7]. A review of fathers' published accounts likewise reported strong positive feelings and personal growth, as well as stressful experiences and negative feelings[8]. The following key themes have emerged from these studies[9].

The gains for families

Emotional gains: Parents and siblings talk about the emotions they have felt and of how deeply the person has touched their lives, including:

– Sharing love with the person;

– Pleasure and satisfaction in providing care for the person

– The person is a source of joy and happiness to them.

Personal Growth: Families speak of the growth they have experienced as a consequence of both the positive aspects the child has brought, and also the struggles of parenting the child. For example:

– A sense of accomplishment in having done one's best for the child

– The child provides a challenge or opportunity to learn and develop

– Having the child has strengthened the family and/or marriage

– Having the child has led to the development of new skills and abilities, or new career opportunities, and

– A feeling of having become a better person - more compassionate, less selfish, more tolerant.

New priorities: A re-ordering of parents' priorities for the better, comes from having the to support another person. This meant:

– A new or increased sense of purpose in life;

– A changed perspective on life, e.g. it clarified what is important in life, and made them more aware of the future;

– Learning to make the most of each day, living life at a slower pace;

– Increased personal strength or confidence;

– Increased spirituality and drawing strength from their faith.

Connected with others: Parent's may develop a sense of belonging to a wider community. For example:

– Having an expanded social and community network through meeting other families in similar situation to theirs.

– Getting to know people working in services and voluntary groups who are supporting their family member

No doubt these four broad types of gains entail many struggles. Without minimising the challenges and heartaches, parents balance them by taking pleasure in the person's development and achievements. It starts from birth as they find out

9

who this little person is and experience the love that flows between them. They begin to see the child as a source of satisfaction, as an object of love and a call to them as parents to change, adapt and grow. This then becomes a major strength in coping with the challenges and sadness that can also arise from time to time.

Such outcomes occur for adoptive parents as well as birth parents. A longitudinal study of families who adopted a child with a developmental disability found that the families demonstrated positive outcomes early in the process and that these effects were maintained over 10 years after the adoption took place[10].

The transformation of what many see as a tragedy into a positive experience happens not only despite, but also through, the care demands the child may make. Mothers who reported higher levels of care needs in their child also identified more personal growth and maturity for themselves[11]. Dealing successfully with challenge, enhances the feelings of efficacy that contribute to personal growth of the supporter.

More fundamentally, this growth arises from the feelings of humanity and love that the child's gifts and vulnerability engenders, as well as from the struggles to meet the needs and from the times of sadness, anger, and loss that may arise.

The experience of siblings

Brothers and sisters too are often supporters in various ways. Their experience may be no less rich and complex than that of their parents, but they may only realise that years later, as Jeanne's story illustrates. She speaks of both the price and the gains that were hers from having a twin brother with autism.

> My life was always about Paul. I was very fond of him because I was really close to him. On the other hand it was very complex because I realized that Paul was a real rival.... I had to know exactly how life was going for him, because however it was going for him, was going to affect my life.

She and Paul shared a common world in a way that Jeanne took for granted when young. She did not see him in terms such as 'autistic' and was quite confused when that diagnosis was made.

> Paul was like a bit of me. I was always more aware of him than my other siblings when I was a child, and I think he was more aware of me. When I was very small my mother couldn't give out to me at all in front of Paul. He would have a tantrum! She could give out to anyone else in the house but she could not give out to me. She forgot we had a little twin thing going. It was just like being able to speak another language, and I can de-code the non-verbal pretty well. I experienced myself like an opposite in that twin universe. Paul is non-verbal and I'm verbal. It's an intimate relationship. It does not depend on speech or even contact in many ways.

Jeanne's whole life was affected for good and for ill by Paul's autism. She felt guilty because she was bright and Paul wasn't. As a teenager she felt bad because she could have a boyfriend and he couldn't have a girlfriend. Everything good she experienced had the dimension that Paul couldn't have this, and that was very difficult. But as well as the sad or painful realities, Jeanne feels she also gained from being Paul's twin.

> On the positive side it made me very sharp at reading human situations and relationships and situating myself. But it also made me hypersensitive to the world around me. In a way I was like a hare checking everything to make sure it was safe.

> A lot of the things I've become are compensations arising from trying to reach Paul in social terms. Basically I'm a very timid person: I was a very timid child and very shy and anything I did like that cost me and to this day it does. I think that I learned from Paul something about reaching way beyond myself because I had to do that to reach him. I've become a friendly, open person in a way, but that wasn't where I started. You could say I have developed that strength because of Paul. And so I suppose I have certain abilities at that level that I gained from a lifetime of reaching Paul, because I did reach him and I still reach him.

Like Jeanne, many siblings have positive things to say about their personal gains from having a family member with a disability, but usually with a price. At times it is demanding and painful, but even then, research suggests[12], there can also be real gains from having experienced a shared life.

THE EXPERIENCE OF SERVICE SUPPORTERS

Service supporters too have a great deal of positives to recount[13]. They make it clear that the richness in their experience does not come from being paid, but comes rather from the humanity of those they support. One group of service supporters generated the list of characteristics they found among the people they supported (see box).

Of course they were not implying that everyone displays these qualities all of the time! Rather it's a reminder of people's qualities that we can easily overlook. Hence it is worth

> **Positive perceptions of supporters**
>
> - Their openness to others, with a non-judgemental acceptance.
> - A sense of presence, living in the 'Now'.
> - A calming influence through their slower pace of life.
> - Naturalness, spontaneity and enthusiasm.
> - Builders of relationships and community: generating loyalty and love.
> - Acceptance and resilience.
> - Trusting and helpful.
> - A willingness to forgive.

learning more about what these service supporters said about their experiences: their own words are very telling.

Openness and acceptance

Anna ran personal development programmes in an adult training centre, and she recalled a recent visit to another centre where she had never been before:

> As I was there early, I went into the canteen. There was one man sitting on his own and I just knew that I could go and sit beside him, that he wanted me to sit with him. He did not give me any particular sign, but there was openness in his body language and energy. There is openness in most people we support: they are not as defended as other people, not as caught with "Who is she now, and what is she going to think of me and what I have to say; and how do I make an impression?
>
> There is great acceptance. You are going to be taken first of all as who you are yourself, not as your role. The encounter is from person to person. The boxes that we put one another in are not there with them. They bring you somewhere deeper in yourself, a place of greater humanity and vulnerability. It's just this whole thing about not feeling threatened, so I'm allowed to be who I am. I have nothing to prove. Is that because of their disability? I do not think so. It's 'nothing to prove' because of their openness and acceptance.

A sense of presence and a calming influence

Anna was also very interested in the sense of presence she found in people, and how this linked for her to important values in her own life.

> They have a presence.... The Buddhists spend years meditating to try and come into the present moment, but our people have it. Now maybe they have it because of a disability, but maybe they're enlightened Buddhists under a tenth lifetime! The Buddhists go on about you're either looking into the future and trying to plan things, or you're stuck in the past and hung up on things, whereas all there is in reality is right now. That is where many of our people are.

Supporters are also struck by the calming effect of people's slower pace of life:

> It's calming, I think because it brings me into the simplicity of now. There is no agenda, nothing to prove, and nothing to argue about. When I sit with them when they are doing art, and they get so absorbed into it, especially the people with autism. On a busy day Sean can be very distressed. You do something calm with him, or when we go into town and sit having coffee, he completely calms down. It's just the ritual of the buns and coffee and he's in his own world, but sometimes he puts his hand here on me and says, "Thank you," and will leave the hand there which is amazing for him. Now that just melts me completely. So there is something about the slowness, the pace, that's extremely deep. It cuts right through all my defences. It goes right into the bone. The pace is slower, and everything slows down.

Naturalness, spontaneity and enthusiasm

Catherine, an arts worker, loved people's spontaneity, but never appreciated how powerful it was until she had the chance to observe those she supported acting on stage:

> Watching actors going out there, not being nervous, loving the stage, no stuff going on – 'What will they think of me?' 'What if I go blank?' 'What if....' They just feel that people would be delighted that they were going on stage because they are so delighted themselves.

Builders of relationships and community

Kieran, a pastoral worker, has a commitment to those he supports that is far beyond any narrow professional definition of his role; such is the depth of satisfaction that people bring to his life. In searching for a way of describing what he meant, he remembered his cousin John Paul:

> John Paul could have ended up in a centre had his mother showed interest years back. Instead he has been working on a farm in the local community - working at being part of the community and claiming his place in the community. Everybody knows John Paul.

> When he wants to work he will, but production is not his agenda. His agenda is being John Paul. In order to be John Paul, he seeks to have a relationship with others. If he's not being productive in the conventional sense, he is productive in calling people to a place of humanity and friendship.

Acceptance and resilience

There is no doubt but that having an intellectual disability at times presents a major challenge and a considerable burden to those we support. The challenges are not only of understanding and learning, but may also include communication difficulties, physical disabilities, and/or social isolation. Overall there may be considerable limitations placed on one's possibilities and choices.

Faced with such restrictions, many people might be expected to become depressed. And while those we support can go through difficult times emotionally, in general they have a remarkably positive outlook on life, as described earlier. Walter is often struck by the resilience and acceptance of those in his Camphill community.

> As a toddler Heather was a slow developer and developed serious epilepsy that responded poorly to all the different drugs. At 17 she had brain surgery for seizures. Unfortunately this was unsuccessful and left her with significant speech difficulties. Recently, however, a new anti-epileptic drug was tried which has finally controlled her seizures. Then, at 26, Heather developed severe rheumatoid arthritis, which has slowly improved with medication.

In spite of all these challenges Heather moved in her late teens from the family home to a life-sharing community and recently into independent supported living. She keeps her home immaculate, sees to her own breakfast and supper, and does her own shopping. She works part-time at the cafe in the local hospital and helps with the cleaning in the community. Her main activity is weaving and she is very accomplished. Her health has not deterred Heather's determination to make the best of her life. She inspires those working with her to carry on with life despite their own relatively minor pains and aches.

A willingness to forgive

Jim has worked in services for many years, sometimes in very challenging settings. His commitment has always been obvious, but he is not a man given to easy sentiment. Yet when asked what touched him particularly in his work, his answer was immediate:

> I am often struck by the generosity of the people I work with in forgiving me or other staff when we get things wrong, or when we have moments of being impatient or even unpleasant. I am not saying that forgiveness always happens regardless, because of course people hold grudges at times as everybody does. But I do see when the person likes you, how quickly they can move on from being upset with you. I am sometimes very moved by that, and grateful too.

> Because of course you don't like yourself if you have been short or a little mean with somebody. It can be really healing when the person nonetheless reaches out to you. It is like as if who you are in that person's eyes is greater than whatever faults you may have, and that you are accepted regardless. Our training textbooks or our service policies do not talk about that, but for me it is one of the most beautiful and hopeful things about my work.

New Perspectives

These assets and gifts of people in need of support are not often acknowledged, even though they are the daily experience of many service supporters. Perhaps they have been consigned to silence because of the dominance of service models that are geared more towards problems and pathologies and the provision of care, than models that emphasise people's gifts and creating opportunities for them. Perhaps the deeper human gifts have had little scope of expression in the prevalent professional mind-sets of paid supporters who are trained to identify and deal with people's problems. We are not trained to celebrate people's capacities. Whatever the reason, it is past time that service supporters should begin to share such experiences with the wider community.

THERE IS THE SHADOW SIDE TOO ....

To highlight family and service supporters' experience of so much that is positive and life enhancing is not to suggest that those they support are seen as somehow perfect in their humanity. Such an idea would imply an offensive 'holy innocents' image that sees them as less than fully human and results in a denial of both their needs and their rights. No less than everybody else, the people we support may sometimes be happy, sad, kind, selfish, open or closed, depending on what is happening within and around them at a particular time, and on how they have been treated in life to date.

As a result, supporting a person can both give deep satisfaction and be very demanding. But in good times and bad, there is always a shared humanity, because those we support are more people of the heart than of the head and generally do not hide either the richness or the rawness of their feelings or needs. Responding either to people's openness and affection or to their fears, angers, or hurts, can only take place through the supporter's willingness to be present and respectful in a way that affirms and gives life. In doing so, his or her own humanity also is challenged and enriched.

Besides, all of us have our shadow side too, as does society as a whole. But we often have far less healthy ways of dealing with it than has the person who is open and direct in what he or she feels. Instead, sociologists tell us, we may attempt to deny our own darkness by projecting it onto those that are perceived as in some way 'different.'[14] They are asked to carry the darkness of society, as well as their own shadow. [15]

In particular there can be prejudice against those who force us to recognise our own neediness and fears. Their obvious disabilities can be an unwelcome reminder of how potentially vulnerable everybody is to sickness or disability. We are never as secure or as in charge as we might like to pretend, and ultimately it all ends in death anyway.

When a society does not wish to face such realities, people like those we support can become the focus of prejudice, causing them to be isolated and ill-treated, even to the point of death. This happened to hundreds of thousands of people with a disability in the Second World War concentration camps[16]. It happens today where life-saving medical treatments are routinely withheld from children with a disability, including those with Down syndrome[17]. It is seen where even those who would normally oppose abortion, find it acceptable where it is likely that the baby would have a disability and is presumed to face a 'very poor quality of life.'

If we are to secure the dignity and place in society of those we support, then supporters have no choice. We must help to draw them from the shadows and declare their gifts and value. In the past, we have all too often failed in this respect. However there are encouraging signs that services and society are starting to get it right. People are seen in neighbourhoods and on television: they are no longer shut away. People are being helped to do things for themselves, and encouraged to be more independent. But above all, people are starting to speak up for themselves.

WHOSE LIFE IS IT ANYWAY?

Living 'a good life' means that one is able to determine the course of one's own life and have the opportunity to create an existence based on one's own dreams, visions, wishes and needs.

Holm, Holst, Balch Olsen, and Perlt, 1996

For generations, well-intentioned services have presumed they knew what was best for the people in their care, and they acted without any consultation or consideration of their preferences. Those they aimed to help often found it easier to comply than to complain. Their own voice was stifled or ignored. Others made decisions for them.

The presumption was that people labelled as having an intellectual disability, were so different that they did not need to have the same rights and entitlements as others in society as they would be unable to exercise them. This discrimination still exists. Prejudicial attitudes live on and will only die out when repeatedly challenged.

The best people to make that challenge are those most affected by a denial of their rights. They know what is important in their lives. What matters to them tells us who they are, and how they must live in order to find personal fulfilment. After all it is their life – isn't it? They want supports that enable them to create ways of life in which they can flourish, including participation in the larger society that is their heritage.

The same messages echo when people are given a voice such as they have in recent reports coming from England, Scotland, Ireland and Croatia[18]. They want:

– To be respected for who they are.

– To be self-reliant and to do things for themselves.

– To have the same choices in their lives as their non-disabled peers.

– To be in control of their lives and determine for themselves what is best for them.

Appreciating and responding to these core aspirations is the hallmark of a good supporter. Let's see what this means in practice, starting with a reminder of the past and a journey that began many decades ago.

THE STRUGGLE FOR RIGHTS

Over the past half century there have been major shifts in how people are treated when they are considered to be intellectually disabled. Today people are living in a relatively benign era, at least in more affluent countries of the world.

– People no longer live in remote institutions; most have been relocated from hospitals and nearly all children grow up in families.

– In most of Europe, their rights to education and to 'an ordinary life' are enshrined in legislation and increasing numbers are joining the workforce and taking part in community activities.

– Official Government policies emphasise social inclusion, choice and advocacy. 'Person-centred services' are the new buzzwords.

– Services seek to promote human development across the lifespan, and much has been achieved by way of new styles of services and creating more productive lifestyles for the people they support.

Yet for very many people there remains a great gap between their day-to-day experience and the well-meaning rhetoric of state policy or the efforts of service providers. Although most people may now experience physical inclusion within their community, they often remain *socially isolated*, despite everybody knowing that our well-being depends on sharing a sense of community with others. It is the quality of our relationships that generates a satisfying quality of life. Often we are so pre-occupied with the provision of high quality *care* in services that too little energy goes into supporting people to become known and valued in their local communities, and providing them with opportunities to live a fulfilling life[19].

In part this stems from societal expectations of people in need of support. These still stress their need for care and protection over the valued contribution they can bring to society. Many years ago Wolf Wolfensberger[20] identified seven well-defined images of people labelled as 'mentally retarded'. These were: a sick person whose life is defined by clinical treatment; a subhuman organism without human rights; a menace to be segregated or even destroyed; an object of pity; a burden of charity; a holy innocent who is less than fully human; and a developing person. All but the last of these are views that have been imposed upon those we support by society's prejudices and fears.

These negative images persist. Whether at the level of policy or in the delivery of services, 'service users' continue to be seen almost exclusively in terms of what they need to be *given* in order to progress, and almost never in terms of what they also can *offer*. Many people find the term and the concept of 'user' offensive, suggesting as it does that they only use services but don't contribute to them. Most are trapped as objects of service delivery. To be seen as agents, instead of objects, means recognising their right to determine their own lives and accepting what they have to offer to others. But rather than being valued, many people are still made to feel ashamed of who they are, and that they should be grateful for whatever supports they might receive, however meagre. Notions of charity predominate over entitlements or rights.

The great challenge, then, facing them and their supporters is how people are not only known and accepted in their communities, but also loved and valued for the contribution that they can make to society becoming a better place for everyone[21]. We can be sure too, that if people are not actively valued, they will most certainly be devalued.

Finally, the 'does he take sugar?' culture also persists, in which others decide on their behalf, usually justified on the grounds that 'we know better'. People are not asked for their opinion, and even if they were, their responses may not taken seriously.

In sum, people with an intellectual disability have experienced oppression in much the same ways as other marginalised groups, such as ethnic minorities. In extreme instances this has resulted in their institutionalisation in mental hospitals, forced sterilisation and even death in concentration camps. Today the oppression can be more subtle but nonetheless real whether it be from individuals, organisations, communities or Governments. Such experiences make people feel inferior and unequal which further perpetuates their submission to the oppressive forces that can be at work in our society.

THE IMPORTANCE OF SELF-ADVOCACY

But these negative attitudes of the past are no longer passively accepted. With support from advocates, increasing numbers of people are fighting for their basic rights with courage and dignity as they slowly overcome their feelings inferiority and inadequacy.

In this struggle for rights, people with an intellectual disability are walking the road already taken by other formerly devalued groups[22]. For them, their journey begins at the margins of society, until a new awareness and assertiveness regarding the injustice of their position leads them to the heart of society as they struggle for their legal and social rights. They define together who they are and develop a pride regarding the worth of their own views and values. This usually occurs through self-advocacy groups, where people develop the confidence and skills to speak up for what they want or do not want in their lives. The support of peers at self-advocacy meetings not only gives great encouragement but also creates a collective voice that is far stronger than that of any individual on his or her own. Their final objective is freedom to lead the life that fulfils people as they see it, and to make their contribution to the wider community.

Barbara Goode, the first lady with a self-acknowledged intellectual disability to address the U.N. General Assembly, put it this way[23].

> Our voice may be a new one to many of you but you should better get used to hearing it.
> Many of us still have to learn how to speak up. Many of you still have to learn how to listen to us and how to understand us.
> We demand that you give us the right to make choices and decisions regarding our own lives.
> We are tired of people telling us what to do, what they want. Instead let us all work together as a team!

The advocacy journey internationally has to be repeated anew in each locality. This means people being facilitated to come together to share common aspirations and concerns. They need support in developing the confidence to communicate their aspirations for change and to challenge injustices. They must be brought into dialogues with the people who hold the purse-strings and decide what supports will be provided. They need to critically review the progress that is made – if any – and not be afraid to speak out.

There is little doubt that advocacy at a national and regional level has primarily driven policy change and helped to create the new styles of support services that exist today. It can be equally powerful for individuals – or can it?

SPEAKING UP CAN MAKE A DIFFERENCE

Joseph had been sent to a reformatory school at the age of three and in his teens moved to an institution for adults. His life changed for the better in his early thirties, when he moved to live and work in the community. Then his life 'went through a bad patch' and he started drinking a lot. He was returned to the institution, twenty years after he left it.

> I was not a happy man. I did not know how long it would be for. Living out in the community is good, and living in here is not good. Here there is nothing for me to do, stuck watching television. I'd like to be out in the community. They tell me they have no place for me. I think myself they don't want me to go. They want me to be stuck in here all my life. I am happy (going to my job every day) because I am out of the place I don't like - the institution. I am still stuck living here, ten years later. Nothing happens. Inside is not a community: it is a sad place.

Joseph made a short film about his life which was shown at a national self-advocacy conference in Ireland. He gave a stirring speech after the showing of the film in which life seemed to be looking up for him:

> They (the services) are understanding what I want for myself. I hope I will be back in the community soon, have my freedom, and be able to do what I want to do. Living in the institution is not right. Everyone should have hope for the future, and life would be better.

At the following year's conference, Joseph gave a one-word update on what had changed for him during the intervening year: "*Nothing.*" There was a stir of anger in the hall and strong condemnations of Joseph's service, which were repeated at other meetings and conferences in the months that followed. Service managers were greatly embarrassed, and while privately they talked of the 'good reasons' why it had not been possible to find Joseph a home in the community, they also said that they were determined that this would change by the following conference. They had been forced to take notice of Joseph's wishes.

Joseph's experience is not an isolated example. Similar stories are often recounted when reviews are held of an individual's person-centred plans. The promises made in response to the aspirations that the person identified some 12 months back, fail to materialise and life for them goes on unchanged and unchallenged. Why does this happen, when we won't put up with such inaction in our own lives?

THE ISSUE OF POWER

Joseph's story and that of thousands like him, is but one example of the powerless people in services feel about having control of their own lives. He had complained for years about his unhappiness in the institution. His service had made sympathetic noises but had done nothing. Joseph himself was not in a strong enough position to demand action. It was only when he advocated for himself publicly and got the support of hundreds of others that the power balance began to shift in his direction. Thanks to what he learnt in his self-advocacy group, Joseph at least had the ability and confidence to speak out. Others, in situations as bad or worse, may have no power at all.

The power people have to make things happen, depends on three things:

- Their personal resources compared to others including their competence, communication, money and friendships.

- The degree to which they are dependent on others for assistance, and,

- Whether alternative arrangements or relationships are available to them that reduces their dependency and offers real choices.

Put this way, we can see immediately that the people we support often have little power over their lives.

For a start, their resources are comparatively limited, not only materially but also when it comes to speaking and acting for themselves. They may lack the skill and understanding to argue their case.

Also they depend on others in so many ways, sometimes totally so. They may be fearful of offending them by taking actions that their supporters may not approve of.

For those living in specialist services, they may find themselves without any real alternatives when their current life situation is unhappy. It is often difficult if not impossible for them to change their service provider. Indeed they may not be able to change support staff whom they dislike and have little opportunity to get the person of their choice instead. They have to put up with what is provided for them – no matter what they want.

On the other hand, supporters have much greater power compared to the person they support. Whether they are family, community or paid supporters, they can control resources and circumstances that are important to the person. They need not depend in any significant way on him or her, and they generally have both work and social alternatives, should they so wish.

But above all of these, there is another factor that emphases the power of supporters. They are expected by society to 'take charge' of those who are dependent. If anything untoward were to happen, the blame would fall on the supporter as they are seen as having the power to prevent the person from harming themselves or others.

Of course, having greater power than someone else is not necessarily a bad thing. It depends on how the power is used. It can be exercised for the good of persons, by enabling and supporting them in every way possible through increasing their resources, reducing their dependency and finding alternative ways of increasing their own power.

Equally power can be mis-used as when it is used to dominate, to enforce control and compliance, thereby increasing dependencies and poor self-esteem. Supporters may not even be aware that they are doing this, so used are they to taking control.

That is why putting in place the laws and systems that support people's rights and give them power over their own lives, has become the key issue in our time for those we support. Only when they are empowered to gain a sense of control over their own lives, will their identity become a confident one, irrespective of any disability they have.

GROWING INTO A CONFIDENT IDENTITY

The emergence of a confident identify can be seen in a new generation of young people who have grown up as part of their society rather than apart from it – the so-called 'integration generation'. They take pride in their achievements – living in their own home, having a paid job, going to College – the list is growing by the year throughout Europe and the world. Each new addition provides another role model for future generations and forces us to stretch our boundaries of what we think is possible.

Nor do the new generation try to hide their disabilities as a former generation was inclined to do when they were relocated from institutions[24]. Their main preoccupation was to avoid getting identified as a person with an intellectual disability. For this reason they avoided association with other labelled persons, resulting in a great deal of social isolation. This is still a reality for many living in segregated services[25].

Once people start to be part of mainstream society and are growing in confidence, they also want to form social groups, have meeting places and share accommodation with friends who share their identity. Like other formerly marginalised groups, they choose to spend their time with others who have similar perspectives and aspirations to theirs. They are unconcerned that doing so would stigmatise them. Instead, they have a confidence in pursuing their own vision of who they are and what is important to them. This development has been seen in noted in Denmark[26] for example.

> We see a movement away from formal integration 'outside' in ordinary society or the ordinary school, towards a more fragmented integration that seeks to retain the opportunities for the disabled to meet each other through the establishment of co-operative housing, meeting places, centres, cafes, and festivals.

Today people proudly come together with others in campaigning or self-advocacy groups, thereby demonstrating the sense of freedom and empowerment that is characteristic of those who had achieved their basic rights[27]. Their representatives may work alongside government officials in planning service provision, they meet with politicians to lobby for more resources, and they argue their case face-to-face with Ministers. Some groups have grown into organisations that provide a range of services for the members, deliver training courses for service staff and undertake their own research and evaluation projects; all done with support if required but through collective leadership. What a difference a generation can make!

 Compass Advocacy Network is a user led and managed group for adults who have learning difficulties in County Antrim, Northern Ireland. They provide information and training and assist members to set up self advocacy groups in their own areas. They also provide volunteers to help members to organise and run their groups. The volunteers support members in learning new skills to empower them to carry out their roles in the groups.

Independent advocacy representation for members is also available through volunteers. Members can request an independent advocate to assist them at meetings, reviews and service planning events. They can choose the person they wish to act as advocate and may change the arrangement if the partnership does not work out.

They have set-up a recycling co-operative and sell goods in a local shop as well as on E-Bay.

They have a drama group that visits schools to make students more aware of what it means to have a learning disability.

An annual conference is organised that brings together advocates from across Ireland.

CREATING A BETTER LIFE

What makes life personally satisfying to us cannot be defined by others, whether family, services or society. Quality of life is not something that is presented to us but rather it is something we actively create for ourselves if given the chance to do so.

Because of their restricted experience, poor self-esteem and low expectations, it may take time for some individuals we support to realise what they want from life, and what they have to offer, but many do achieve this. As their confidence grows, then what is personally important to them becomes clear, regardless of what others may think. This means giving them the space and the opportunities to express their desires and ambitions.

In recent years various studies have collected the views of people with intellectual disabilities in different countries[28]. This has been done through people meeting in groups, or in interviews or by completing questionnaires. A remarkable consensus emerges from the findings as to the priorities people hold for their lives. Admittedly, these are the views of more able people who can speak up for themselves but it is just as likely that they apply to people with more severe or profound disability who may not be able to express themselves as clearly.

We might use the apple tree of life as a means of illustrating the fruits they value. But these fruits are only possible if there are healthy roots that enable the tree to thrive. Hence we also need to identify what it is that helps people to flourish.

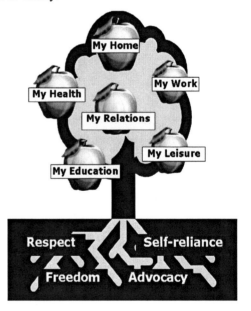

The fruits of life

My relationships: People placed great store on their relationships with family and friends, and with their support staff. They spoke of the loneliness they experience and being socially isolated. Having a boyfriends or girlfriend was mentioned as well as the opportunity to marry.

"Friends help you to get your rights – they help if things go bad."

"People are not encouraged to be in relationships by families or staff"

"We need more opportunities to start small and before going to the boyfriend-girlfriend stage".

My home: They spoke about having a place of their own; of living in the community rather than in special centres or homes; of choosing the people they lived with; of being in a safe and pleasant neighbourhood convenient to facilities, and of playing their part in household tasks.

"People want a choice of independent living options."

"I would like to share with my girlfriend maybe sometime in the future."

"I want more independence and privacy but I need staff to help me with the cooking."

My Health: They recognised the importance of keeping fit and leading healthy lives. They wanted equal access to health services and for doctors to tell them about the treatments they were given. They knew the pain associated with the death of loved ones.

"Doctors don't listen, they just look away and talk to someone else like the staff."

"I can't read the information on tablets – there should be pictures or symbols".

"I lost my mother last year – I think of her every day."

My Work: Opportunities to undertake productive work were frequently mentioned, preferably in paid employment. They felt the attitudes of employers needed to change. The rules around social security allowances prevented people for getting paid work.

"Getting jobs is hard outside of the workshop."

"I go to lots of job interviews and don't get any of them. Employers don't want to employ disabled people."

"We're not getting enough pay for the work we do."

My Education: They wanted opportunities to learn and to be trained in skills that would help them to get a job and more generally to do things such as handling money and travelling independently.

"I missed out on secondary school – there was no bus to take me."

"I want to get into a training course that leads to real work."

"We need to know more our entitlements and speaking up for ourselves."

My Leisure: They wanted to know what was going on in their local community and to be supported to join in the activities that interested them on a regular basis. They spent too much time in the home watching television.

"I want to mix with other people in the community."

"How about more discos and clubs that we can meet our friends safely."

"I like to visit my relatives at weekends".

The roots of life

Throughout these findings there are some deeper themes; the roots that are needed for the person to flourish and produce the fruits that people cherish for themselves.

Respect: They wanted to be treated as adults who can be trusted with responsibilities. The hurtful attitudes of others and the bullying they had experienced proved to them that prejudice still existed in their community.

"Treat me as me!"

"People should consult me about what I want to do or I think should happen."

"We're called names when walking passed teenage gangs or groups outside of pubs in town and cities".

Self-reliance: People wanted the chance to do things for themselves – being independent was how they put it. Commonly given examples were managing their money; going out with friends and having privacy.

"If I didn't have needs I wouldn't be in a group home but I can still do things for myself."

"I have to hand over half my money and I manage the rest but I could manage all of it."

"I wish I could learn to drive."

Freedom: People wanted to break out from the control they experienced in their lives. This meant having choices – so they could make their own decisions – and having control over the things that are important to them, such as how they spend their money and their relationships with others.

"It's our own lives, it's our decisions!"

"Having a relationship must be a person's choice."

"I have no choice which staff come to my house; I get on better with some than others".

Advocacy: They wanted their rights to be recognised and to be supported in obtaining their rights. People felt they should be consulted rather than told what to do. Their confidentiality should be respected and private matters should not be discussed with other people.

"We need to let the public know that we're no longer to be treated badly."

"People need to stop putting themselves down".

"It's OK to make a commotion if you're being treated unfairly"

As you will no doubt have noted from reading these lists, people's aspirations for their lives are little different to those we hold for ourselves, which is yet further evidence of our shared humanity. But what is very different are the many obstacles they experience in trying to fulfil these aspirations. In part these derive from the impairments that they may have been born with, which affect their capacity to learn and develop. But more crucial are the barriers they encounter within a society that denies them the opportunities and supports required to experience a good quality of life. The remainder of the book describes the supports people require in order to surmount their impairments and reduce the barriers they encounter.

OUTCOMES OF SUPPORT

The fruits and roots of the apple tree of life serve another important purpose. They provide the yardstick against which the support we offer people can be judged. Put simply, have we improved the quality of their life?

Today there is greater appreciation that supports have to be judged in terms of the outcomes they produce for the people supported[29]. The core questions are ones like these: have we helped people to live where they want to live; to be productively occupied, to have friends and to be treated with respect? Outcome-based evaluations are a stringent test of the investment we make in supporting people. Some would argue this is too demanding because of the other factors outside of the support service that can affect these outcomes. This is true but in response we would contend that is not just the attainment of the outcomes that are important but rather it is the focus for learning that they offer about what helps and hinders their accomplishment. These insights should energise the service to improve the supports it offers to people. And should this not happen, outcomes do keep the focus on the person being supported.

By contrast, service providers have been judged mainly on the 'inputs' they have delivered to people – the number of support hours a person receives; the availability of special therapy, the new facilities they have opened and so on. More recently the focus has shifted towards *how* the support was provided and regulations were enacted by governments that defined the quality of the care offered in state-funded residential homes and day centres. The link between the quality of care and people's quality of life was presumed rather than examined[30].

Re-appraising deficits

One further point is worth noting in what people say about their lives. Although they acknowledge their limitations, these do not dominate their thinking in the same way that health and social service staff tend to talk about their needs. They are more inclined to focus on people's deficits and differences rather than their talents and aspirations. They focus on poor health, challenging behaviours, attention deficits, mental health problems ….and so on. Much time and effort is spent on assessing and treating people's problems. Granted it is right and proper that people should get the specialist support needed to address their difficulties, but this emphasis cannot dominate the way people are supported, for two reasons.

- Their problems are likely to be acerbated by the poor quality of life they experience at present[31]. Hence enriching their daily lives must be an integral part of any treatment approach and is certainly necessary for bringing about sustained improvements.

- Effective treatments for many health issues are built on boosting people's self-esteem, self-control and self-confidence while helping them to acquire more positive behaviours to replace the negative ones that hold them back[32]. Focussing only on the latter is not sufficient.

Person-centred

The summary we have presented of people's aspirations provides an overview of what they generally think will enable them to live more fulfilled lives. But it is crucial that we focus on individuals and assist them to define what is particularly important for their life, now and in the future. Admittedly it is not always easy for people to speak up for themselves or to make known their hopes, fears, desires, concerns, dreams and limitations. Yet our own personal advocacy helps to test out the realities of who we are and the opportunities that life can offer us. Crucially it also enables us to garner the support of others in fulfilling our aspirations. Thus the greatest support we can offer to people is with their own advocacy. In Chapter 3 we will explore more fully the means for doing this through the personal relationship between a person and his or her supporter.

THE ROLE OF THE SUPPORTER

It is a sobering thought that the finest act of love you can perform is not an act of service but an act of contemplation, of seeing. When you serve people you help, support, comfort, alleviate pain. When you see them in their inner beauty and goodness, you transform and create.

Tony de Mello

Various supporters share in people's lives to varying degrees, whether as a family member, a community supporter, a friend, a volunteer, or a paid supporter. What is asked of each supporter depends on the degree of involvement she or he has with the person.

In this chapter we examine the common features of a supportive relationship. First we will describe the different elements that make up the support role and outline the basic attitudes supporters need to bring to these relationships. While many do this spontaneously, we think that all supporters benefit from being aware of what's needed to deepen their own relationships and to mentor others in being more supportive.

Paid supporters can face particular challenges in creating the type of relationship we have in mind, yet outside of family members, they have the greatest potential for influencing a person's life. Hence the second part of the chapter focuses especially on them.

EXERCISING THE SUPPORTER ROLE

The elements that contribute to being an effective supporter can be summarised as follows.

An expectation of growth and development in the person supported

Unless there is the expectation that people will continue to develop throughout life, there will be little consciousness of the kinds of support they may need, or how to enable them to fulfil their potential. The supporter who expects growth will find, nurture, and celebrate it in little things as well as big.

A commitment to good communication

Good communication is essential to all relationships. It is the way in which people find out what is going on for each other, including their feelings. Otherwise we only have guesses, even fantasies, which may lead to all sorts of mistaken assumptions. In particular we can get stuck in negative views that lead to damaging interactions.

Supporters can have diverse challenges in learning to communicate better with a person whose communication is limited. If they are to get to know and be known by the person, they need to work at improving their own communication.

Taking your lead from the person

As the very name suggests, a supporter has to be behind, beside or beneath the person helping to keep him or her afloat if you like, but certainly not pushing or pulling them. It's the person being supported who moves things along, while the supporter is there to provide assistance and gentle guidance as needed. This may mean for example, encouraging them to take decisions and to do things for themselves, or boosting their confidence and use of initiative. The goal is to support the person to be his or her own man or woman.

No faultfinding or blame

Criticising and blaming people are damaging responses to the difficulties that arise in relationships from time to time. Instead, the basic attitude called of supporters is that of seeking to understand the message being given by the behaviour and looking at the context in which it arises, including the key relationships in people's lives. This attitude of mind also makes it easier for supporters not to take things personally and reduces the likelihood of a power struggle developing within the relationship.

> Dorothy was an intensely jealous and controlling person and created many
> turbulent scenes for no apparent reason. Some supporters disliked her deeply

because of how she treated others. They became punitive and dismissive in their attitude towards her and were less willing to offer positive supports.

After a dangerous assault on a housemate, Dorothy was moved to live alone in an adjoining apartment. This was for safety reasons, but the effect was immediate. Removed from the constant presence of those who made her jealous, Dorothy became calmer. She still had outbursts, but her supporters learned to leave her until they would be welcome back. When Dorothy wanted support she got it, otherwise she was content to be alone to do things that interested her. She was developing an independent identity for the first time in her life. She joined the local self-advocacy group and loved to go to training activities and conferences.

Dorothy continues to be a rather prickly lady with a bad temper. But her life is now more fulfilled, and she is generally a happier person to be with. No longer a dangerous misfit, she has earned herself a new respect.

Dorothy's story shows that blaming somebody resolves nothing. By learning from her, supporters came to see what she needed and sought to offer it, with great results. Had Dorothy always been 'heard' in this way, years of misery could have been saved for all concerned.

A duty of care

A supporter, who is asked to stand alongside people in a co-operative as opposed to a directive manner, has at the same time a 'duty of care' to ensure they come to no undue harm[33]. The balance between respecting people's wishes for their lives and taking steps to ensure their safety can be a delicate one. We need to be very aware that we don't project our fears on to another person. Particular sensitivity is required when there are concerns that the person may be caught in an exploitive relationship that nonetheless is very important to him or her. Respectful channels of communication are crucial at such times, allowing the person to discuss what is going on and to hear the supporter's concerns. Of course the supporter must act where significant exploitation is taking place. But where matters are less clear, the person may need to learn to be more assertive so that exploitation becomes less likely. The duty of care is not just about dealing with the big matters, but also about teaching the person how to take care of him or herself. We will examine this issue on more detail in Chapter 9.

The recognition of boundaries

Because their relationship with people may be strong and mutual, it is essential that supporters be clear about boundaries and never take advantage of the person supported, either emotionally, financially, or sexually. People's vulnerability can mean that a supporter may slip into mild forms of exploitation that become habit-forming and which could further weaken boundaries over time. Some supporters have a professional code of ethics[34]. Others need access to best practice guidelines and mentors who enable mutual relationships and promote appropriate boundaries.

In essence, the role we are defining for supporters is in some ways new, but in other senses is as old as humanity. Throughout the generations, people have supported each other at times of particular need. The supporting function is an extension of an established relationship (the formation of which we will describe in Chapter 4). Throughout, the supporter respects the personhood of the individual but balances this against his or her presenting needs. In many ways the supportive relationship expresses humanity at its best. Both parties grow and benefit from the shared experience.

THREE BASIC ATTITUDES OF A SUPPORTER

The creation of a supportive relationship depends on three basic attitudes which make up the mind-sets that supporters need to bring to their role:

An understanding by supporters that their primary teachers are the people they support

This is true in a number of ways. First of all, people's very being teaches the supporter what it is they need and what they can offer, in order to fulfil themselves. By really paying attention, supporters learn to exercise the skills they have, and to develop new ones, in order to offer the range of supports the person needs.

Secondly, because they live close to their own humanity, people needing support are natural teachers of the heart. Ongoing contact with that humanity deepens the humanity of their supporters. This can be particularly true for those supporters who have previously been somewhat cut off from their own emotions.

Thirdly, many people being supported show great personal faithfulness to their supporters. They can be very patient with the one who is still not getting it right, or not showing appropriate respect, or not recognising their needs. As Joan says:

> It is like as if, out of their long experience of being supported, the people are saying, "What are we going to do with this new person? How are we going to help him or her become a better person and therefore a better supporter?" Our desire to help may be authentic but the ways we go about it can be so inappropriate. To keep their own lives tolerable, the people have to train supporters in, whether consciously or not

A willingness to grow in self-knowledge

Whether they like it or not, supporters regularly face truths about themselves arising from situations they have to address. Self-knowledge is a key tool in the supporter's bag that makes it possible to be aware of aspects of the self that may be unhelpful or even damaging to the other person, if left unchecked.

At the end of a tiring day in the shops, we were discussing where to go for something to eat. Mark wanted Chinese food and the others took up the idea with enthusiasm. My heart sank: I was very hungry and had never found Chinese food particularly filling. Rather than accepting what everybody wanted, or at least being honest about my own preference, I asked Peg if she would not prefer a burger? Probably I picked Peg because she is good at giving the answer she thinks a supporter wants. The tide was definitely turning in favour of burgers and Mark had grown silent, when we were joined by the team leader who cheerily asked, "Right then, where are we going to eat?" "Chinese" said Mark, quick as a flash! Everyone nodded, and off we went, me rather begrudgingly.

When I thought about it that night, I felt ashamed of my selfishness, but was particularly upset to realise how ready I had been to manipulate people in order to get my own way. It was painful, but at least I had become more aware of my need to work on not imposing my own agendas on the people I was supporting.

Supporters need to have this kind of awareness of how they are doing in the job, particularly when the work is demanding. The supporter who is unable to name what is happening inside him or her self is unlikely to understand or respect what is happening to the person being supported. A reflective attitude of mind is essential if creative responses are to be made to issues arising[35]. This capacity for self-reflection is central to self-development for the sake of the development of others.

The undertaking of continuous self-development for sake of the development of others

Because one's humanity is the primary instrument in supporting another person, the supporter is asked to go on developing personally in order to become ever more able to support the development of others. In Joan's view,

Each of us must be in touch with where we need to grow; based on what you learn about yourself from the people you are supporting, and make a commitment to grow for the sake of the work you are doing. If you are too blocked, the person supported does not get the kind of relationship that is needed, or the kind of help.

Joan had found that her own most significant support relationships were those that asked her to grow, such as those with Melanie and Anne, described earlier.

The most significant relationships are not necessarily always positive. Even the difficult relationships that end up broken and sour can still be terribly revealing and 'growthful'. I can think of other people that I have a nice relationship with. But there isn't a big "I really relate to this person, we are growing together" or a big investment on my part. The person could move on, and I'd certainly say, 'I'm sorry you're going.' But there is not a big sense of loss. The significant ones are where something has been touched deep down that leads to growth.

Everything we have written thus far applies to all supporters and we stress again that many come to this role with the necessary mind-set and appreciation of their key functions. Their intuition and sensitivity are valuable gifts to be treasured and celebrated.

Although every effort may be made to recruit paid supporters with these qualities, in practice it may turn out that some lack a spontaneous appreciation of people and enjoyment of their company, or may have a blaming attitude, or may not have a fundamental belief in people's potential. The role of the service leader is crucial at this point, ensuring supervision and mentoring for the supporter and offering training that aims to increase responsiveness to the personal and social needs of those they support. But in the end, a supporter that fails to respond positively to people's relationship and community needs should not continue to be employed.

A NEW MEANING TO A PROFESSIONAL RELATIONSHIP

Whether working for a organisation or employed directly by the person or the family, paid supporters are the most important personnel in any service system because of their role in helping to form and deepen relationships in people's lives, thereby addressing their emotional and social needs as well as giving practical supports in daily living. Everybody else in the wider service system is there to support that core role, as managers, administrators or specialists.

Some readers may feel nervous at the ideas we outline for the paid supporter's role. They may be concerned about people becoming over-dependent on paid supporters. Or they may fear that the role would be compromised if supporters become emotionally close to those they support. They prefer to define their role by their professional functions and leave it at that. As we have argued, these functions, though important, are insufficient to achieve the aspirations of modern services. A new understanding is needed of the professional support role.

The person-supporter relationship is not a usual social friendship, because the supporter is paid and the person may have little choice in the matter. Nor is it the kind of relationship we have with a medical doctor, for example. We are willing to be in the patient role for short periods, but we would object greatly if asked to spend all day, every day, being related to as somebody's patient, especially in the privacy of our own homes. Remember that people and their various paid supporters may be together up to 24 hours a day, seven days a week.

Another image we have to reject is the employer-employee relationship, where the supporter is employed by the person to give the help needed to make life feasible. It is certainly essential that the supporter realises he or she is there to do the job as the person wishes, rather than believing oneself to be the boss. But beyond that, it is hard to see the relationship as that of employer and employee, given the particular needs of the role and the very personal nature of the interactions between the pair.

If it's not a social friendship and not the usual professional-client relationship, and if the employer-employee model is not an adequate fit, then how is this kind of bond to be described? We propose that it be understood as *a support relationship – a particular and most important relationship.*

The person-supporter relationship has to be genuine, reflecting empathy and care within the minutiae of each day. The primary instrument is always the supporter's own self, his or her own humanity, bringing understanding and skill in relationship development between the person and the supporter, and then more widely into social and community networks. This is the central responsibility for which the supporter is being paid. And in all of this, the supporter's own satisfaction is also an essential outcome for the continuation of the relationship.

Rather than being a threat to professional roles, relationships are a primary means by which professionalism is fulfilled. Fear of creating over-dependence on service supporters does not mean denying the great value of that relationship: it means rather that other, unpaid relationships must also be nurtured.

Dignifying support relationships also means that terms that are often avoided in services, such as 'love' or 'affection', become as much part of everyday language as the more objectifying professional terms in common usage. Cathy knew what to call the experience when she first encountered people in her summer job.

> What I remember most clearly, and what brought me back to this work, was the fact of a love experience, which I felt deeply – sensing for the first time that I could have a deep effect on another person, looking forward to being there, thinking we are going to have a good time.

> People's vulnerability also touched me. All Gerard could do was laugh or cry. He literally could do nothing for himself. He particularly touched me because he was so totally vulnerable. That was like a call to me. If I did not make sure his pillows were straight or that his pyjamas were on, he could not ask for it or do it for himself. I wanted to be there to do it. I knew that I loved the people in that place.

Many paid supporters could describe experiences similar to Cathy's, although this may never be discussed in these terms in service settings. Like thousands of others, the writers of this book have been greatly enriched by those we have supported. We chose this work not only to answer people's needs, but because we found in them a richness that was attractive and nourishing, a humanity that has kept us committed down the years.

Personalising daily activities

Some paid supporters may feel that there is not enough time to be personal with people because there is so much to be done in carrying out expected daily activities. Supporting such activities does not preclude relating in a close and loving way. Awareness of both elements is needed.

> We get caught up in the practical demands so quickly – one way or the other hung up on them because that is all we know how to do, or because it is more comfortable and protects us from our own vulnerability. Or because we come from a professional background and we think that is our main gift.

But it is not a matter of either/or. Doing essential activities and experiencing loving relationships intertwine in the simple business of each day. Cathy referred to this as amalgamating the programme with the personal. As in any home, it is through the big and little business of each day that people encounter and relate to each other. The programme and the personal are not just complementary: they are the same thing.

The paid supporter as an enabler of community

Supporters also need to be effective bridges between the people they support and the wider community; a theme we will pursue in Chapters 6 and 7. If supporters do not believe that those they support offer something valuable to others they won't pursue opportunities for them to meet and mix, and the public will find it hard to move beyond fear, indifference, or misunderstanding. Even for their own sakes, especially if working alone, supporters need that community interest and involvement in the life of each day.

An unhappy outcome of professionalisation is the clear separation that many supporters maintain between work and their personal lives. Few, for example, use their own social network to help integrate people into the local community. While it is understandable that supporters need a 'non-work' life as well, there is something uncomfortable about that sometimes total separation. After all, many of us mix and socialise with work colleagues and their partners or family in our free time.

A great contrast often exists between the narrow range of supporters' role in the work setting and the leading roles many play in their local community and various organisations. At work they may be treated as if they cannot be trusted with significant decisions and resources, while outside they show many capabilities.

RELATIONSHIPS AND POWER

We saw earlier how the power balance in a relationship depends on the relative resources of each partner, on the degree to which a person is dependent on others, and on whether alternative relationships are available. We can see immediately that those we support often have little relationship power. Their resources are limited, they depend on others in many ways, sometimes totally, and they may not be able to remove or even distance themselves from a disliked supporter.

This power imbalance is added to by having a supporter who is expected to be 'in charge' and make sure nothing goes wrong. Finally, the supporter also has power by virtue of not having a formal disability, therefore having freedoms, possessions and skills that can seem great to someone who has so little[36].

Those who have the greater power in a relationship can use it for good or for ill. The difference between destructive power and positive power is that the first is exercised through dominance, the latter through co-operation.

The negative use of power

The constant dominance of another person is abusive behaviour[37]. It is easy to see this in extreme cases, when people are physically assaulted, verbally humiliated or sexually abused. But it can also exist in more subtle forms that are corrosive over time. Small but constant criticisms and frequent if seemingly mild undermining of a person can amount to serious bullying. If correction pervades all aspects of a person's day, it becomes a burden that diminishes rather than enhances the individual.

As well as doing harm to the person that is being controlled, the destructive use of power also damages the humanity of the person who is controlling. It creates resentment and fear, so that people distance themselves as far as possible. A supporter who is not respectful will damage not only that other person's humanity, but also his or her own.

Positive power

Positive power can be exercised only through co-operation, because you cannot force people to fulfil themselves. As we have said, it begins with a willingness to listen to people – their words, moods or actions, to learn who they are and what matters to them. Supporters must be open to learning the other person's worldview and wishes, and present their own point of view in turn. It is then possible to offer the kinds of support that would be helpful.

Where people lack the natural impulse towards life-long development, they need help in discovering their capacity for self-fulfilment and the pleasure it can bring. A supporter's creative caring seeks ways that will help people to grow. Positive use of power means offering oneself in service – using one's intelligence, gifts and heart to help other people become who they are meant to be.

Of course there are times when something has to be insisted upon, for the good of the individual, but the approach has to be a respectful one.

> When asking David to do something regarding his personal hygiene, which was awful if you ignored it, I would say, "David, we have discussed this, and I know you feel you have good reason for not wanting to wash yourself, but it has to be done because otherwise people will avoid you and you will damage your health." So there is discussion involved, and I try different approaches, maybe trying to jolly David along, or asking what his lady-friend will think of him if he smells. But if the only response is obstinate refusal, there is a need to insist, and I will.

Issues of power exist for all supporters in their relationships with those they support, whether we wish it or not. These issues come and go at different times, depending on the circumstances. When we become stressed, we can resort to dominance in an effort to manage a situation. Particular people bring out our tendency to control, especially if the individual is in some way challenging, or reminds us of somebody we do not like.

All through our careers as paid supporters, we need to be conscious of our power and seek to use it positively. Many supporters do that in a wonderful way, but it takes constant vigilance as it is so easy to take control of their lives, when people have little experience of speaking up for themselves.

PROMOTING ADVOCACY

We want now to overview the various ways supporters can encourage the advocacy of people they support[38].

Personal advocacy

At its simplest, promoting advocacy means listening to the person and striving to understand the deeper meanings in what they say. The Box gives some helpful advice to new supporters on how to get to know the people they will be supporting.

Getting to know the person

- Take time to talk to the person over a period of weeks, even months. Look at photograph albums with them; ask them about their family background; have them tell you stories of things that have happened to them in the past and talk about how they see the future unfolding for them.

- Help them to create a 'This is My Life' scrapbook that will assist new supporters to know more about them.

- Read what is written down in records and reports about the person and add to these any significant information you glean from your own conversations with them.

- Accompany the person to different places and see how they interact with different people. Supporters often comment on how they see 'another side' to the person when they are with them on holiday or a visit to the family.

- Observe the times and places when the person seems 'at their best' and also when they appear to be 'down'. Reflect on why this is so and what this tells you about their support needs. Check these out with the person and other supporters.

- A summary can be compiled of the crucial things that supporters need to know about people with severe communication difficulties and the main ways in which he or she likes to be supported. For example, it could give information about how they communicate; their likes and dislikes in food and drinks and any bed-time routines.

The phrase, 'person-centred planning' is often used to describe the process of working alongside people to elicit the goals and pathways they want to pursue. Various tools[39] are now available to assist supporters in helping people in describing their hopes and aspirations, and for planning the particular forms of support that will assist in achieving them. Central to whatever approach is used is the ethos of people taking control, ownership and responsibility for their life in an informed and healthy manner while also taking account of their vulnerabilities.

This sort of planning is a developmental process; one that grows the more it is exercised and it may take years to refine and come to fulfilment. Undertaking regular reviews is one helpful means.

> Moraig is the leader of a supported living community. She says: Person-centred planning really works for us. The person invites the supporters he or she wants to be present. This can include family members and friends as well as supporters from different services. He or she is the focus of the meeting and will be present throughout even if verbal communication is limited. A facilitator usually helps with the organisation and smooth running of the meeting and aims to create a relaxed atmosphere, respectful listening and a sense of togetherness.
>
> The person who needs support sets the agenda. The group listens as the person shares his or her hopes, concerns, complaints and needs. Everyone is free to contribute their insights and experiences, emphasising the person's strengths as well as their needs. The meeting moves on to draw up a plan for the supports that the person requires. Everyone is encouraged to dream and not be overly constrained by the possible obstacles. This includes the contribution of family, friends and community supporters as well as the service and specialist supporters.
>
> The plan is mapped out on large sheets of paper using pictures and drawings and is later written down in an 'easy-to-read' format. The plan belongs to the person but all the supporters are given copies.
>
> By having these different people present at the meeting, it is easier for everyone to get to know one other and who is doing what. However it may mean that planning meetings need to be held at evenings or at weekends.
>
> The same group come together once a year to check on how things are going (or more often if people wish). In this way supporters are accountable to the person and to each other as to whether the plans were carried out and any necessary adjustments can be made.

Group advocacy

There is danger though, that amongst a team of supporters the voice of the person gets diluted. The idea of self-advocacy groups provides the opposite context: the members outnumber the supporters. People supported by a service can be encouraged to come together as a group so that they can discuss issues of importance to themselves. These groups provide a sense of solidarity when there are common issues to take to supporters and the services that employ them, so for example, supported living schemes have created tenants' committees. Service managers will meet with the committee on a regular basis to hear their concerns and proposals for actions. They will also report on how concerns expressed at previous meeting have been addressed. Training needs to be made available for self-advocates and opportunities provided for them to meet with more experienced self-advocacy groups.

Independent advocacy

A third approach is independent advocacy[40]. Supporters can direct people to an advocacy service who will support the person with a specialist issue on which supporters may have insufficient knowledge, for example, the social security benefits people receive or relationship difficulties. There may be instances too when people want to complain about the support they are receiving from a service or when major changes are being proposed and they lack someone to speak up for them. It is more appropriate for an independent advocate to take this forward than a supporter employed by the service. In addition to mainstream advocacy services, such as Citizen Advice Bureaus, specialist advocacy services for people with disabilities are becoming more common, although ongoing funding remains a problem for them, as can their reliance on finding volunteers who are prepared to act as independent advocates.

Whatever form advocacy takes, it should pose no threat to supporters, as some are inclined to think. It is not a question of fault-finding or apportioning blame, not should it result in confrontations. Rather the essential purpose is to gain a greater insight into the needs of the people we support and to create a sense of solidarity in achieving common aims.

THE CENTRALITY OF GOOD COMMUNICATION

In essence advocacy is about giving people a voice. Yet communication is not always easy with the people we support; many of whom have difficulties in communicating through speech. Some cannot talk clearly and others may not talk at all. They may struggle to understand what is said to them while giving the impression that they do. Those having difficulty communicating are reluctant to speak unless spoken to or they depend on others to speak for them. Frustrations may be mutual. Supporters are inclined to give up or speak instead to others with whom they can communicate more readily. But the good news is that given a positive attitude and the use of certain skills, communication difficulties can be overcome. Two things need to be kept in mind:

Everyone is a communicator

First, that every human being – no matter how disabled – is constantly communicating. We need to 'tune' into the various ways they could be sending messages to us.

We are all born with an innate capacity for communicating with one another, and humans never lose those early forms of non-verbal communication. Eye contact, body language, gestures and tone of voice are used constantly by everyone throughout life.

These non-verbal signals are said to be the most honest form of communication because often they show our true emotions[41].

So communication is more than speaking. We need to be aware of, and use, other methods. Something as simple as facial expression can say so much. So too can touch, a caress or a punch! Eye contact and our body language lets others know whether or not we are listening to them, and if we are relaxed or uptight.

If we assume that people are trying to communicate with us, then we will try to communicate with them. This in turn makes them try harder and so a virtuous circle develops of ever-improving communication and relationship building. Here's how Joan's communication difficulties were overcome.

> Joan was born with poor vision, decreased hearing and spastic limbs. As a child and adolescent she was very unhappy and angry, often hitting her head against a wall and poking her eyes. When she moved to a therapeutic school community, everyone's aim was to make contact with her and to encourage her to relate to others and to the world around her. The 'problem' behaviours lessened.

> Joan's eye contact is non-existent but nevertheless people hold her hand and look at her while speaking. They tell her in simple words what is happening. If she is agitated, they sing to her and gently stroke her face. At the very least Joan learns she is not alone, that there are people around her whom she knows and trusts. But Joan may understand more than we think, so people tell her what's happening, what's being done to her and by whom, and where she is going. Sharing such information might seem pointless to someone who questions Joan's ability to hear and understand; but that misses the point of relating to her as an independent adult, according her the dignity of a human being and doing everything one can to facilitate a relationship with her.

Adapting our communication to the person

Second, able communicators need to change their means of communication to suit the person needing support. It is easy to label the other person as a 'bad' communicator – but how does that help him or her? What if you thought of yourself as the bad communicator? The trick then is for you to do better by adapting your communications to the person's needs. We do this naturally with people who speak a different language to us and whose knowledge of English is limited. We use simple words and gestures in the belief that we can get through to them if we try another way.

Exactly the same approach can work with people we support. The starting point is to think ourselves into their position so that we can appreciate the need to adapt our means of communication.

Claire works in a day centre with people who are profoundly disabled. Here's her take on communication.

It is not hard to build a relationship with the people I work with. You are working on body language all the time – facial expression, that kind of thing. It takes a bit of time, but not much more than with other people.

When I came back to work this afternoon, I was sitting on the floor beside a girl who has a severe learning disability and autism. She had only been with us a few months and always sits on the floor, so if I want to be near her, I sit there too. She always smiles and seems to enjoy it and will let me play with some of the bits and pieces she carries around in a little basket. I was just thinking to myself that this girl fascinates me and that I would love to be able to get into her head for a day or spend at least an hour a day on a one-to-one with her. I suppose it is this curiosity about people like this girl that makes me want to stay in the job.

COMMUNICATING WITHOUT SPEECH

As supporters the onus is on us to find ways of communicating with people who do not depend on speech. There are many ways of doing this, formal and informal[42]. For example, music can provide a means of relaxing together; likewise singing and story telling build a sense of togetherness. As we speak we can use gestures, facial expressions and body language to make clear our meaning. We can learn to read our partner's signals, enlisting the help of others if necessary.

We can use photographs to recall people and activities and identify individuals' needs and wants. Picture Boards can enhance two-way communication, using pictures or symbols chosen to cover the person's basic needs; for example, toilet, TV, drink, and yes/no. By pointing at pictures the person understands better what you are talking about and can tell you what they want or how they are feeling.

Modern technology offers other possibilities. Voice synthesisers say the words when a symbol or picture key is pressed. The number of symbols can be increased so that people can 'talk' in simple sentences. This means they can ask questions, request things and tell you how they are feeling.

Or we can learn sign languages which were originally developed for people who are deaf, but have also proven valuable with some hearing people who cannot speak. Speech and Language Therapists advise on the alternative methods most suited for use with particular individuals and offer training and support in their use.

However these communication methods only work when there is commitment from supporters to make them work. It takes extra effort to use a sign language or communication board. They don't always yield immediate results. But they do give a 'voice' to people who otherwise cannot communicate. They increase the likelihood of them connecting with other people and forming a relationship. That is why it is crucial for everyone in regular contact with the person to augment their spoken word with signs, pictures or other symbols.

NURTURING VERBAL COMMUNICATION

Service staff and people with intellectual disabilities were asked what was meant by social inclusion. Staff felt it meant using community amenities, knowing neighbours or having friends. The people themselves mentioned these things too but for them, the most important thing was people talking to them and not ignoring them!

Abbott and McConkey (2006)

Verbal communication is arguably the greatest human attribute. It opens up so many opportunities to forge relationships with others. A dearth or deficiency in verbal communication deprives people of many of these opportunities. Hence every supporter's priority must be to nurture verbal communication.

Hearing

Verbal communication depends more on hearing than on speech. We often presume that people are hearing us clearly when they are not, especially if in a noisy place. A hearing loss is sometimes called the 'invisible handicap'. Other explanations may be invented for failure to hear – "*they are not paying attention; too wrapped up in something else*". If a problem is suspected, especially in older people and those with Down Syndrome[43] – hearing should be checked out.

Active Listening

The onus is on the supporter to be an 'active listener'. We need to create opportunities when we can listen to one another without interruptions. This can happen informally over a cup of tea, when out on a walk or on a car journey. The setting you choose can also put people at ease.

We need to show we are listening to what they have to say by giving our full attention. We need to encourage any faltering effort, to work at understanding what they mean, and not jump to conclusions or put words into their mouths. And most important of all, we need to allow them time! We may need to ask them to explain again or to ask questions to help clarify that we have understood. We can summarise what we have heard and check it out with them. People can be encouraged to reflect on what they have said or asked to come up with ideas for solving the problems that concern them.

Nor should we shy away from people expressing their emotions. Time to cry or be angry may be needed before a person can move on to more positive topics. Such 'heart-to-heart' sessions may not arise that often, but we all benefit from having someone with whom we can have such conversations. If supporters are not prepared to do it, people may have no one to whom they can turn.

Making clear your meaning

Listening actively is but a first step: people may also need support in working out the meaning of what is being said. This is similar to the assistance you provide when talking to people who know only a little English. You do not need to talk like this all the time, but it is important to do so when you really need to get your message across. People we support can be very good at persisting in this!

> Carol came to me one morning before Christmas, saying what I thought was 'tea' and pointing to the front of the cafe. "Yes, people were drinking tea," I said but she shook her head and said 'tea' more forcibly. "Do you want tea?" I asked. More vigorous head-shaking and hand gestures followed; her hands pointing up as in prayer. "Is it something to do with keys?" Obviously not – because I was then taken by the arm into the locker area, where Carol produced the Radio Times with a Christmas tree on the cover and said, with exasperation in her voice, what I now clearly heard as 'tree'. "A Christmas tree for the cafe?" I guessed. Her smile showed we had connected at last and when she pointed to herself saying, "me do", I knew who wanted to put it up!

Encouraging people to talk

Conversations are based around turn-taking, with an equal share of listening as well as talking. Each responds to what their partner has said rather than just talking about their own concerns. A starting point is to find topics of mutual interest or an activity that you can do together, but even then supporters may need to change their style of communication when conversing[44]. Some tips are given the box.

Taking time to converse with others helps relationships to gel. It can be too easy to give the impression that we don't value a relationship because we are busy doing more important things than chatting. But the 'spin-off' is that the relationship is strengthened. This then enables us to converse more freely, which then further strengthens our relationship, and so it goes on.

Roles and relationships

The way we communicate with people speaks volumes about our relationship with them. Supporters who make time for conversations in which they are active

> **Tips for conversing**
>
> - Be more responsive during conversations, with more use of nonverbal feedback in particular; such a head nods, facial expression and gestures. These all indicate that are you listening to what the person has to say.
>
> - Ask open questions (What do you want to drink?) rather than closed questions (Would you like some milk?)
>
> - Talk about yourself, what is happening in your life, what you think and so on. Leave time for the person to react before moving on to another topic.
>
> - Follow your partner's lead: build on what your partner says. A simple technique is to repeat what they have said with a questioning intonation. This may entice them to say more.
>
> - Do not be afraid of silences. Sometimes being with people is sufficient.

listeners will be perceived as different to those whose communication is mainly directed at getting people to do things through giving orders. Directive speech is necessary sometimes but if persistently used it results in a relationship that is more akin to that between a boss and a worker or a teacher and a child[45].

Hence the roles we take on as supporters determine our style of communication. We may model ourselves on the way we have seen other supporters behave without thinking through the consequences. It is helpful to reflect on which roles are most typical of a relationship and what they do to your communication style.

Consciously adapting our communication to suit the people we support is a major step in reframing our relationships with them. But often we are unaware of the way we talk to people. That's why communication training courses may ask people to make a video-recording so that they can hear and see themselves. In essence our message is simple. Be flexible in the way you communicate if you want your relationships to flourish. Choose the manner of communication that best suits its purpose.

An example for others

Supporters can be a model to others by explaining why they use certain approaches and encouraging others to improve their communication. It is also important to point out what is good about their present communication and not just focus on what needs changing. It can help to have notes that summarise methods that are helpful with particular people, or to organise awareness raising or training courses. Thankfully there is much that we can do to enhance people's communication. The starting point is not other people changing – but being willing to change ourselves and adapt our own ways of communicating.

THE GAINS FOR THE SUPPORTER

Supporting others is not just about giving. As noted in Chapter 1 there are many gains in knowing and appreciating the people we support. Affirmation becomes a natural impulse that infuses life. Anna, a long-time support worker summed up the overall impact on herself in this way:

> The effect that the experience of knowing people over many years has on me is that I hugely want what is good for them. It really engages me, motivates me, and makes me want things to be right for these people. I want to see them valued and appreciated, because I have experienced something of who they are and what they give to me.

It is important that as supporters, we talk about our positive views and experiences, and know that others share our point of view. Together we are redefining the presumptions underlying the term 'intellectual disability' and what people so labelled can contribute to others. The focus now needs to be on the gifts and capacities of those we support, and on the tangible contributions they make to human communities.

Being in tune with them holds the possibility of nurturing our common humanity, because we are open to the gifts they offer. Supporters who are not open to mutual relationships can be destructive of that same humanity, as happened so often in the past. But appreciative supporters who form deep bonds can enable people to fulfil the potential that their lives hold for themselves and for others.

THE DEMANDS ON PAID SUPPORTERS

Yet as well as giving many satisfactions, being a supporter can make high demands. Cathy summarised her experience in one house as follows:

> I felt challenged to the hilt. Liz was terribly self-destructive, taking even the most fleeting opportunity to slam her head against the wall or gouge her remaining eye. I was afraid of her, not because she was going to do anything to me, but because of the distress she could cause me. I grew to dislike her so much.

> The experience of my helplessness was terrible. I had no way of trying to influence her. Physically I could stop her of course, and often did, but I could not build the relationship with her that would allow me to say anything that would stop her. I had no comforting words to reach her with. So, the self-destruction was happening in front of me. Professionally I did everything that was required of me, but at a personal level I felt very broken.

The demands in supporting Liz are heightened because much of this work takes place in groups where individuals need varying degrees and types of support. When someone like Liz goes through a difficult time, the desire to support may be swamped by frustration, anger or a self-protecting instinct to reject.

> I really felt faced with my own limitations – and that is not just words from a book! I really was: I found myself really frustrated in front of certain people – really impatient, very quick to become angry. And seeing that in myself I felt I was a failure - that I was not good enough to be in this work because I have these awful feelings about this person.

The experience of such ambivalence is normal. Where there is no ambivalence, neither is there a real relationship. But supporters need support in dealing with the parts of themselves they would rather not look at. Most have high ideals regarding their role. Where anger or hatred arises, guilt and confusion can follow, because such feelings are at such variance with self-expectations.

> I tried to deal with that by becoming hyper-efficient. Looking back, I can see I was afraid to slow down, because that left me facing my helplessness. But the busier I became, the less present I was to people in the way that I wanted to be, and which was the reason I came into this work in the first place!

If not supported, the outcome can be 'burn-out' as supporters seek to be only the 'good' self, at great personal cost. Or they can withdraw emotionally from those supported, in order to avoid frustration and failure. Worst of all, they can end venting their negative emotions on the person being supported[46].

All this can be further complicated by ways in which personal experiences and behaviour patterns affect what supporters expect of themselves, as Joan found.

> I always tend to think there must be something I'm doing wrong. This is part of how I was brought up. I was led to believe that my father's wellness – he was an alcoholic – depended upon me. That was a most unfortunate thing to believe, but it continued right up to the day he died – that his very being depended on me. If he was drinking, indeed if he died, it was because I did not do something or other.

> There is still a residue of that in me. I think in my work that there is something I did not do, or something I did wrong. I'm not really very free in that yet. I need to be able to say, "Hey, you did your best, what more do you want?"

Supporters may have to cope with constant strain in settings where verbal or physical assaults may occur. The great dedication and decency shown by most supporters in such situations is often taken for granted or even unnoticed. Scant attention is paid to what they need themselves if they are to continue to be a healing presence for others. In Joan's view,

> People are not prepared enough for what happens, do not realise how deeply this work will touch on who they are themselves, for good and ill. And people are not accompanied well enough. There is no preparation. No follow-up. No 'What you are going to experience when you are here.' What to look out for, what to recognize as being good, what to be careful of... There is not enough in place when things start to get difficult.

SUPPORT FOR SUPPORTERS

In order to fulfil the role, supporters too need support, from their colleagues as well as through more formal support systems[47]. In Chapter 8 we will look at the kind of organisational culture within which these supports need to be offered, but here we are focussing on the various personal supports that need to be available.

Mentoring

Supporters can benefit from regular chats with a more experienced colleague about themselves as a supporter and team member. A wide range of topics can be discussed although the focus is usually on the supporter's feelings and any particular highpoints or difficulties encountered. The mentor's role is a sounding board – helping the supporter to reflect on his or her experiences, and together thinking of how they could adapt their supports to the person. It may also be a time to tell a supporter to ease off and not to expect too much of him or herself.

While much of this may be done informally, individual supporters should also have formal opportunities for their work to be reviewed with the team leader[48]. This gives leaders an opportunity to emphasise the core values that underpin the work and to identify ways of providing further help to the supporters, such as attendance at training courses. It allows each person's strengths and contributions to be named and praised. It is also a time to identify any weaknesses, but with a view to deciding a positive course of action for dealing with them. The aim is for all supporters to feel affirmed and valued.

Support groups

Support groups can be very helpful, where those working together give time to being reflective in a respectful and accepting atmosphere. It takes time people to feel safe to share what is happening on that interface between their professional and personal selves. One service found a hopeful way of doing that.

> Every two weeks we gathered in the sitting room of one of the houses. The team leader began with an input about our work together and our shared successes and struggles. Then there was silence that was allowed to continue for some time, as people reflected on what had been happening in their work since the last meeting. Someone might then share about a moment or event that had been particularly touching, focusing on the human gains and pleasures that it brought. But difficulties are also acknowledged: the sharp moment of anger or hatred towards a very demanding person needing support; how hard it is to bear particularly distressing aspects of the job; the feeling of being so utterly drained at times that it seems one has nothing left to offer.

The service supporters greatly valued these sessions, but some felt that more was needed than time to share what was hard, or what was particularly good, this past week.

> We don't have a place where people are learning what it means to be an emotional being, what it means to be angry, how to spot when somebody is uncomfortable, unhappy, upset, how to deal with somebody who is having a hard time dealing with somebody else? It is not just how you are getting on; it's what is transpiring at an emotional level. We are not being taught, or teaching each other, how to grow in the emotional areas.

> A service can be a place of personal growth and even healing in big or little ways, for the person that is open to it. It is a matter of a sufficient degree of understanding that helps a supporter through difficult personal or interpersonal issues that may be triggered by something arising within their work.

An employee assistance programme

Many services offer an Employee Assistance Programme to supporters who are having personal difficulties. This may be because of stress arising in the work – whether from supporting very demanding people or from bullying by a colleague or boss – or because of personal struggles, family and marital difficulties. The employer pays for initial sessions so that they can access outside professional assistance.

Crisis support

A supporter can be traumatised following a physical assault or due to working in a high-stress environment, and may need de-briefing and support. This is particularly important where supporters are asked to go on seeking a positive relationship with the person who assaulted them rather than reacting by becoming distant and punitive. Services need to provide designated people to offer that support, which may include seeking medical assistance or counselling as well as arranging substitute staff if the trauma is such that the supporter needs to go off duty. The Assaulted Staff Action Programme is one example of a formal crisis support programme[49].

Finding time for oneself – stress and relaxation

No matter what supports a service puts in place, supporters have to learn how to look after themselves. This means knowing one's limits and how to rest and relax. Regular exercise is particularly important, and some find supports such as massage or reflexology particularly helpful. Joan found such supports essential, as was time to listen to music, to visit family and friends, and to give herself treats. Holidays away as often as she could also recharged her work battery.

Sharing the support role

The pressures on individual supporters are much reduced when other caring people are also available. This can come through working in teams and by linking with others such as family members and community volunteers, and being part of social networks and community organisations. In Chapter 8 we will take up this theme in detail.

We have focussed at length on supporters in this chapter because an understanding of their role and the skills with which they exercise it, are crucial in order for them to carry out their core function of nurturing mutual relationships with the people they support and with other supporters. In the next chapter, this is theme which we will examine in detail.

NURTURING MUTUAL RELATIONSHIPS

Relationships with others lie at the very core of human existence. Humans are conceived within relationships, born into relationships, and live their lives within relationships with others. Each individual's dependence on other people - for the realisation of life itself, for survival during one of the longest gestation periods in the animal kingdom, for food and shelter and aid and comfort throughout the life cycle - is a fundamental fact of the human condition.

Berscheid & Peplau (1983)

Some things are so much part of life that we can take them for granted, like the air we breathe or the meals we sit down to every day. Relationships can be like that. It seems perfectly natural for most of us to have people who share our lives, who care for us and for whom we care. Our time and activity is closely woven into the lives of others, and so much of our satisfactions come through that shared living.

From time to time we are jolted out of this security. We all know loneliness at some time, maybe when we move to a new place to live, work or study. We settle only when we form significant new relationships. We feel sad for somebody whose life is obviously lonely. But it is when we experience the final loss of a loved one that we realise how much our lives are defined, expressed and enriched with and through others, and how greatly life is changed by the ending of an important relationship.

Even without experiencing such a loss, we don't have to reflect long to find how hugely important our relationships are to us. A group of paid supporters attending a training workshop surprised themselves by taking just a few minutes to come up with the list of what relationships bring to us (see box).

What relationships bring us		
Love	Support	Affection
Trust	Encouragement	Fun
Sharing	Understanding	Listening
Thoughtfulness	Respect	Security
Friendship	Honesty	Companionship
Human Contact	Re-assurance	Interest in Me
Happiness	Challenge	Fulfilment

This listing shows that we are all experts when it comes to knowing what we receive and give in our relationships. One supporter wondered aloud *"Why did I never apply all this to the people I work with?"*

Every word on the list is powerful, which is not surprising. Our lives would be almost unimaginable without that constant group of people with whom we share the ups and downs of each day. We were not designed to go through life alone: we depend on one another in so many ways, practical, emotional, and social. We were not meant to be completely self-contained.

It is both the need we have for each other and our desire to share that draws us into relationships. If we have good relationships, then some time alone can be enriching and helpful. But if we are too much alone, we feel incomplete, painfully so if it continues for a long time. First emotionally and then physically, people can grow sick and even die of such loneliness. Children fail to thrive and adults sink into depression and self-neglect. This is not a matter of choice or a personal failure. It is part of our human nature.

WHY RELATIONSHIPS ARE SO IMPORTANT TO US.

Relationships create the human closeness that nourishes and supports us.

When we have good relationships we feel alive and fulfilled. We are nourished by those who love us, in a manner as real as the physical nourishment of food. Closeness to others brings warmth and security. It is as if we have found our place humanly speaking, both because we are cared about and because we care for others. We belong.

Elizabeth was a quiet and rather withdrawn woman, preferring to spend time on her own reading, listening to music or watching the TV. When Paul moved into the house it became obvious after a few months that a friendship was developing: Elizabeth blossomed - her mood lifted and she became much more sociable, spending a good deal of time with Paul, but also joining in activities with others in the house. Eventually, when her parents commented on the change in her, she was able to admit to them how happy she was in this new friendship with Paul.

Relationships bring people into our lives with whom we can share our interests and activities.

The pleasure we get from life is generally greatly increased when we share it with others. This is true in the simple things as well as the major events of life.

> Eamon is an outgoing man, well known in the town where he lives. Regarded as something of a 'good luck' mascot at the local soccer club, he goes to all the home matches and has ready lifts when the club is playing away. He does not limit himself to soccer, however, and is to be found at all sorts of public events, helping with stewarding or being his own one-man welcoming committee. For many people such occasions would be incomplete without him, such is his place in the local community. He loves returning the greetings he gets everywhere he goes.

We are greatly stimulated when we can share our enthusiasms. The very act of sharing deepens our ideas and interest.

We grow and develop as humans through the give and take of relationship.

We long for relationships not only because of our need but also for what we want to express towards those we love. That is not to say that giving in relationships is easy: it is often a struggle, depending on what is being asked and on our mood at the time! But certainly close relationships challenge us to grow as caring human beings, and to put others before ourselves.

> Anne has a craving for coffee that borders on addiction. She has to eat her meal before she has her limited amount of coffee, because once tasted she refuses any further food or drink. She has to be encouraged to eat slowly, as she wants to bolt her food in order to have coffee, and is likely to vomit. So when eating with her, Malcolm has to be aware of Anne's needs but at the same time, he finds her eating habits distasteful. In order to support Anne, he has to ignore his own instinctive feelings. Through his commitment to Anne he finds he is becoming more tolerant.

When someone knows and appreciates us, we come to know and appreciate ourselves.

Friends and family act as mirrors where we can see ourselves, according to the way in which they respond to us. When other people obviously like us, we can more easily like ourselves. When the messages they give affirm us, we grow in confidence. When we are accepted despite our failings, we can accept ourselves and know that we don't have to be perfect to be loved. Because others care for us and appreciate our caring, we know ourselves to be valued.

Martin was abused at home and an outcast at school. He lashed out at those around him when upset, but beat himself more often than he attacked others. His supporters were endlessly patient, giving repeated reassurances and showing such affection as he would allow. It was difficult for all concerned, not least Martin.

Martin was coaxed to try sports and he proved good at the javelin. He became proud of his physical prowess and delighted in showing off his muscles, a breakthrough for a young man who had believed nothing good of himself. He became a World Games gold medallist and enjoyed the attention that followed. While still highly insecure, he would now prompt paid supporters to tell visitors about his medals, and he glowed at the telling before retreating once more into isolation. Social events remained difficult. But he gradually became more secure and able to take part.

The four points just outlined give some sense of why relationships are so crucial, but on paper they are a rather tame expression of the depth and urgency of our emotional needs and capabilities. Our very identity is formed through the tapestry of relationships in our lives. Without them we cannot know who we are, or appreciate our place in the world.

An emigrant, who has a sense of her ethnic difference or 'strangeness' mirrored back to her by those she meets, finds it difficult to develop a sense of belonging in her adopted country. If it continues, her primary self-image will remain that of 'emigrant.' Only when invited into relationship with those around her will things change. The same happens if those we support experience themselves primarily as a 'patient' or 'client' or 'service user', rather than having opportunities to learn and express who they are through ordinary human relationships with the people who share their lives.

RELATIONSHIPS ARE EVEN MORE CRUCIAL FOR SOME

In fact, relationships are even more important for the people we support than they are for people without formal disabilities. This may seem an exaggerated statement at first sight. Relationships are so utterly crucial for everybody, how can they be more than crucial for any particular group?

We need to explore this claim in depth, for if true, it intensifies the already very powerful demand that relationships be viewed as the most important capacity and need of those we support. We begin by examining the four primary sources of affirmation that we all have, and then reflect on these affirmations in the lives of the people we support[50].

FOUR SOURCES OF PERSONAL AFFIRMATION

How do I know myself, express myself, and find my life to be of value? Most of us have four broad ways by which we answer these questions – through our effectiveness, our possessions, a sense that life is meaningful, and our relationships.

Effectiveness

Our effectiveness is a major avenue of affirmation and fulfilment. We are able to do things and have an impact in our personal world, however big or small that world may be. We can be good in our jobs, create a home for our families, enjoy leisure pursuits, and contribute to our local community. We experience ourselves as able to bring about change for the better in our own lives and those of others. In this way we come to know and develop our abilities and have the satisfaction of using our talents. All this gives us a sense of personal worth and leads to the recognition of that worth by others.

This is no less important to people we support. Many are proud of what they accomplish and this contributes greatly to their self-esteem. But equally they may get repeated reminders about what they cannot do, about their *ineffectiveness*.

This can happen in a well-intentioned manner, as daily life is punctuated with frequent corrections from those supporting them in a tone of voice and to a degree not experienced by others once childhood is past. Even a well-meaning family can perpetuate the experience of ineffectiveness. "You cannot do it: I will do it for you." The clear implication is that the supporter can do it better, faster, and more efficiently.

Much worse are the dismissive or stigmatising messages people get about themselves from society because of what they cannot do. Their perceived 'ineffectiveness' causes them to be excluded from shared activities, because they are not seen as able to make a worthwhile contribution. As one young man wrote of his sister:

> A lot of her friends are becoming teenagers and are leaving her behind as a little girl whose mind won't grow older. I guess you can understand her loneliness now. That is nearly the only thing that makes her sad.

Self-esteem can be damaged repeatedly by their own and others' response to their limitations and by unfavourable comparisons with peers and siblings.

Possessions

The possessions that we gather are another way people use to feel good about themselves. Whether a room or a castle, our home is an extension of who we are. If it is a place that we like, we feel good about it and by association, about ourselves.

Most people have possessions of which they are proud, either because of their material value or because of their status value. Sport trophies, citations, or whatever - are often placed where they can be admired. Likewise we keep possessions of sentimental value, because they remind us of a happy time, a valued relationship, or a past achievement.

As well as the pleasure of having them, using possessions furthers our self-satisfaction. Because we have a car, a boat, a fishing rod, a garden, or whatever, we can engage in activities that are fulfilling. They broaden the ways in which we can express ourselves and offer opportunities for activities that further our sense of effectiveness.

Possessions are likewise important to the people we support. Many are proud of their satellite televisions or i-pods, or may feel good because of the clothes they wear. But in general many cannot gather the material or status rewards that would symbolise their worth to society. Most are badly paid or depend on social security; few can take ownership of prized possessions such as a car or house. Their exclusion and low status means that such rewards are not available to them. Their self-respect suffers.

Meaning

We all need to feel that life means something. Unemployed people may struggle when days seem empty and society seems to say that their contribution is not required or valued. A parent can feel a similar loss of meaning when the children are raised and gone. Whatever our age, we need a sense that life has a purpose.

Our effectiveness and possessions contribute to that sense of meaning. Rearing a family is central to many people's lives. Meaning may be found in being committed to a worthy cause, hence religious belief is an important source of meaning and security for many.

All these elements can also give meaning in life to those we support and this should be nurtured. But many people may not experience a clear purpose to lives and they find fulfilment more in the here and now, particularly in their relationships with others.

Relationships

As already discussed, relationships are the primary means by which we find fulfilment and affirmation[51]. Our growing identity depends on continuity and nurturing of our primary relationships. Throughout life, our happiness comes from positive relationships.

Those we support are extremely dependent on relationships as the primary means (sometimes the only means) of knowing themselves, expressing themselves, and finding themselves good. This is because their effectiveness is limited and their possessions are few. Nor can they find meaning in life through the abstract concepts that society values, such as status and esteem. The greater their need for support, the more absolute is the individual's dependency on relationships.

Looking again at the listing of what relationships bring us at the start of this chapter, it is troubling to ask how many of the people we support experience these gains from their relationships. Do they know a consistency in love, in friendship, in understanding, in sharing, in listening, in companionship, and so on, in the same way and to the same degree as we desire for ourselves?

Even many of those who live in places where there is genuine care and kindness may not have stable relationships. Most are still overly dependent on paid supporters and limited family contact, and have few if any friendships outside of the service. Such loneliness can be true of people living in the community settings as much as those in old-style congregated housing and institutions.

The loneliness of never being needed

But the loneliness of people who lack stable relationships is not only because of what they do not receive, but also because of what is not asked of them. If we were never asked to give to others or made to feel needed, we would feel unwanted and useless. It is the give and take of relationships that asks us to grow. Indeed people needing total support who are responded to with obvious pleasure, whose smiles are regarded as a gift, whose vocalisations are reacted to – learn that they bring something precious into the lives of others. They unerringly sense that they are valued and loved.

Many people we support do not have their social and emotional needs adequately met, and accordingly they may not easily come to know themselves, express themselves and find themselves to be of value. How are they are to be supported to find the relationship they desire? Let's look at what we know about the development of mutual relationships.

STAGES IN FORMING MUTUAL RELATIONSHIPS

Relationships don't just happen: they take commitment and work. For that reason, and because they are crucial for those we support, it is important to understand the stages in relationship development. These evolve smoothly in many cases, but difficulties may arise that need to be addressed if the relationship is to grow. A relationship is a complex bond between two people that operates on many levels, some quite hidden[52].

Our focus here is on the supporter and the person supported. In a later chapter we will look at relationships among friends. We review five broad stages in the development of a relationship. We all experience these stages in our own lives but perhaps without being aware of them. But for a supporter to be effective, it is important to understand the process as two people start to get to know one other. We explain why it can be a challenge to forge a relationship with some of the people we support, and how to respond to it.

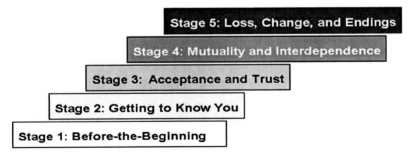

Figure: Stages in building a relationship

STAGE ONE: BEFORE-THE-BEGINNING

How any two people approach a relationship between them depends on each other's expectations, attitudes and beliefs. These will be shaped by their particular history and their past experience of relationships. Where experience of other people has been mostly positive and hopeful, particularly in childhood, there is a good possibility that a new relationship can develop, provided the other person is likewise open and respectful.

Some of the people we support are wary of relationships due to hurtful life experiences. Some have known rejection or have been violated by abuse. Trusting others is difficult for them because such trust was shattered in the past, leaving the person angry and suspicious. Self-esteem is poor and there is fear of further hurt.

Burton Blatt[53], pioneer of de-institutionalisation, told the story of a paid supporter and an out-of-control five-year old with cerebral palsy and no speech. For weeks she lashed out furiously while the supporter sought to reach her, ignoring her behaviour and continuing the routine designed for the security and growth of all the children. The child watched and it was obvious that she wanted the supporter to be angry too, because the child would know how to relate to that as it fitted her previous experience of adults and of life.

> One day I was particularly tired and discouraged and she must have sensed something amiss. Spilling milk is not unusual in a pre-school situation, but our little firebrand made a last stand. She threw her milk at me with deadly accuracy. I sat stunned for a minute. As the milk dropped from my hair, I deliberated – one false move could undo everything. I felt an angry tear in my eye. She looked at me, her face red and contorted with emotion. I didn't move. Suddenly she staggered from the room. Still I sat, knowing I must take some action. A few moments passed. She came running back into the room, hands dripping with wet paper towels. I didn't move. She smoothed back my hair and wiped my face and clothes with erratic, awkward hands. She had suddenly dissolved into a compassion she failed to comprehend because she had never needed it; it was a brand new experience. Involuntarily my arms went out and she flew in.

Far from seeking relationships, then, some may initially actively reject contact with others. Paid supporters are particularly important for such a person, as they are together over time and may gradually break through the barriers and find the form and degree of relationship that the person can cope with. Supporters need to value relationships for such people as long as they cannot do so for themselves.

But in our experience the great majority of people are open and eager for relationships with their supporters, and with the world in general, if only others can be equally open and responsive to them.

Lack of skills in making relationships

We must also acknowledge that some of the people who need support have disabilities or conditions such autism and its associated sensory and social difficulties that can make it harder for them to relate to other people. It is also important for the supporter to make allowances for this. People may find it hard to acquire the social skills that facilitate relationship development, such as understanding turn-taking in conversation. But having all the desirable skills or understandings is not a pre-condition for a relationship. Rather, the development of such abilities may happen *through* relationships over time. Helping some people to achieve these skills can be challenging and may take a lot of time, but is a key role for the supporter.

Supporters' prior experiences and expectations

Equally supporters' preconceptions and past experiences can determine the relationships they have with people who have been labelled as 'needing support'. Needs and fears influence supporters too as they approach a new relationship. Happily, many supporters have the experiences and talents to be caring individuals who relate warmly to others. But at times, any of us may be inhibited by the hurts of our own history and may take personally the way the people they support react to them.

The degree to which we are able to answer to the emotional needs of those we support depends on a variety of factors:

— *Our personal openness* to caring and relating. This may vary according to our own relationship experiences, especially in childhood. We may be less open to relationship with others than we might wish, and supporting people who can be so direct about their feelings can be both an attraction and a threat.

— *Our image of the people we support* – whether we see them as fellow humans with the same emotional and social needs as ourselves, or as 'different' and somehow 'less human' because of the support they need. Also some people gain a 'bad' reputation that can cause some supporters to treat them in a manner that excludes the possibility of a positive relationship.

— *Our understanding of our role* as it relates to the emotional needs of those we support. Professional training programmes, hopefully in the past, may have stressed that one must retain a professional detachment from those we support. Or we carry over ideas about our role from previous workplaces that discouraged relationships. Or a conflict arises between what a supporter believes is important and a supervisor's priorities.

— *The social and professional support (or pressure) from peers*: where the attitude and examples of other colleagues is positive, relationship development is supported. Equally peer pressure may inhibit the development of relationships if others perceive such efforts as an implicit criticism or threat, or as favouritism towards certain individuals. Similar the encouragement of managers is vital.

— *The service ethos, structures, and supports*: where these operate in a manner that respects and values the people in the service, their families and supporters, there is a far greater chance that supporters will behave in the same way.

Thankfully most supporters bring a great deal that is positive from previous life experience and many of those we support have a talent for relationships that can make it easy to connect and relate. Nonetheless, it is important to realise that what happens as we approach a new person is greatly influenced by past experience, and that we are meeting not only that individual but also the impact left by major figures (or lack of major figures) in that person's past and in our own.

STAGE TWO: GETTING TO KNOW YOU

Introductions

People need to be introduced to one another. Formal introductions signify respect for both parties, each of whom has an unspoken question from the outset: "Who is this person to be for me?" The answer is important for people in a service because supporters play a major role in determining their quality of life. The supporter too is wondering about the history, satisfactions or challenges each new person may present.

An emphasis on the person's strengths reduces the likelihood of negative first impressions. A welcoming celebration of some sort, signifies the valuing of the newcomer and creates a pleasant occasion that helps everybody begin to get to know each other in a relaxed way. As one supporter commented:

> My first impression was of the friendly atmosphere that was embodied in somebody like David, who welcomed me and chatted – talks your head off really! But things like that helped me feel that people really wanted me to be there.

The development of relationships is also influenced by temperament. Some people are outgoing and spontaneous and have a heightened gift for friendship. Others are more introspective, and while their capacity for friendship is no less, it may evolve in a slower and more cautious manner.

Attractiveness is another characteristic of relationship in this stage, including a compatible sense of humour. Agnes recalls her first encounter with Michael.

> It's hard to say what attracted me, because a lot of people were not fond of working with him because he could be messy at times. I heard people saying this in front of him one day and I said "Don't mind them Michael, I think you're lovely." With that he jumped up on me putting his legs around my waist and his arms around my neck. He made it quite clear that he understood what was being said about him and that he appreciated somebody being on his side. I enjoyed time with Michael because I liked his company and enjoyed the activities that he liked."

Spending time together

For a relationship to develop people must spend time together. We usually choose who we spend time with socially. This may not be true for people who come into each other's lives in the context of support services. But two people cannot *not* relate, for good or for ill, once placed together. This lack of choice creates both difficulties and opportunities.

> When I first met Matt I thought here was a man who has nothing to offer. He was not attractive. He was disagreeable. When I first met him, he snapped at me, and would not talk to me for ages. He was awful. I did not want to be near him.

> But over time, we began to have nicer moments and would chat. I used to say things like, "Let's sit down and talk about how you are doing." But as I got to know him, I realised this was presumptuous of me. I was half his age and yet was treating him like a child. It amazed me the way he and others tolerated that. He heard me laugh at the wrong things even at very sensitive times. He is a man who forgives people day after day. I gradually discovered that Matt is a tremendous person and I love him deeply. He is all heart.

It helps for people and their supporters to engage with each other in different settings, not just when support is provided and where expectations and roles can be quite fixed. Getting to know somebody when sharing an activity in a leisure setting, for example, can allow a new sense of fun to enter the relationship. People can listen at a different level and gain new insight into each other. This can happen in particular where people go on holidays together and get to know each other in a completely different way.

Weighing each other up

From the beginning, people are unconsciously weighing each other up. They may find each other attractive, interesting and entertaining, or may feel a need to be cautious, or may even actively dislike each other from the beginning. They begin to exchange 'sample' interactions by which to evaluate each other, seeking answers to unspoken questions such as

- Who are you?
- What can we offer each other?
- Can I trust you?
- What do you want from me? Do you ask more than I wish or feel able to give?
- Can I risk showing you my hurts and failings, without being rejected by you? Will you accept and like me, just as I am – my limitations as well as my strengths?
- Is there hope that we can grow to care for each other?

The answers that people believe they get to these questions over time will determine whether mutual acceptance and trust will begin to develop.

STAGE THREE: ACCEPTANCE AND TRUST

The building of relationships into the third stage happens through the ordinariness of each day, doing what needs to be done while always seeking to be attentive to the human quality of what is taking place. While special times of nurturing and sharing are important, it is the consistency of the experience that someone cares about you that builds trust and a sense of being valued. Joan put it this way:

> Take teaching somebody how to bath. It's not just one, turn on the tap, two get the towel; it's an awareness of who this other person is, and who I am as a person that is involved in there too. It is not just about a physical task, but about the messages you are giving in the way you go about it. If you are teaching people to wash their bodies, what are you saying by the way you touch them, by how you are in the bathroom with them? Even somebody who doesn't speak or is totally dependent wants the dignity of privacy. How you treat me in those personal tasks is a reflection on how you see me as a living human being.

> In effect you are either saying "I value you; I know you are trying your best." Or you are saying, "For God's sake why can't you put your hand out in front, I'm fed up with you not doing it right!" In your impatience, you give the message that you're fed up with the person not just with his or her rate of learning.

It is this merging of the personal with the daily routine that gives infinite opportunities to develop and deepen the relationship. When given messages of acceptance, people gradually reveal themselves to each other as they judge that it safe to do so. Areas of deepest vulnerability will be the last to be shown, and could even be defensively expressed in some form from the outset, by challenging the supporter or withdrawal from contact. But where there is acceptance and hope of affirmation, trust gradually grows.

Testing the Relationship

People will test the authenticity of an emerging relationship if past experiences taught them that people couldn't be trusted[54]. Those who have greatest reason not to trust may be most extreme in their acting out. They may feel driven to show their worst side to see if the other person will still be there after seeing how awful they can be. This means that the times the supporter experiences as the most difficult, may in fact be the most important to their relationship, as we saw in Burton Blatt's story, above.

If the person finds commitment in the supporter, then the relationship has the potential to be a healing one. The supporter is asked to continue to show respect and caring, to see the humanity and the cry behind the angry façade, and to go on believing in the person and the possibility of him or her opening to a new and nurturing relationship

Joan came to realise that Anne was afraid to let her real self be seen: her endless challenging kept Joan at bay, while at the same time demanding her constant attention.

> The psychologist felt that Anne was dealing with me in the way she wanted to deal with her mother. This became very evident when a place came up in a more independent house. Originally she had no choice about leaving home. Now she acted out the difficult choice about moving on. She wanted to show that she was grown up, but she was afraid.

> Finally she decided that she would ask about the vacant place. While waiting for an answer, there was still a lot of going back and forth. "What do you think? Do you want me to leave?" It was like "Mummy, will you let me go? Mummy do you still want me?" I was saying, "Anne, it is what you really want." I was being a parent saying, "You can do it, go for it." In the end, she did. She is so proud of herself now!

Very often the dynamics are not as complex as those with Anne, but they may be nonetheless demanding for that. For example, Eddie displayed challenging behaviours when toileting – smearing and trying to spit at and slap the supporter's face. Many things were tried and failed. Finally two people always went into the toilet with him and held his hands so that he couldn't hit or smear, and put a towel across his face so he couldn't spit. Agnes described what she did when Eddie came into her group.

> I didn't want this big negative session a few times every day, so I decided to have a go at something different. I decided to go it alone with him and leave out the restraining and the towel. I would say nothing during the whole session because it wouldn't have been good, and no matter what he did, I was going to give him a hug before he left the bathroom. This was going against everything I ever learned about reinforcing good behaviours, because here I was going to reinforce a load of bad behaviour as Eddie loved to be hugged. I told no one because I didn't want to be locked up! I went through a few months of real hardship, maybe less. I kept no records because I felt the whole thing was so crazy. Then Eddie's behaviour began to change. He settled down and learned to tolerate the session and it was no longer the traumatic episode that it used to be for him.

Recognising our common humanity

We all have our limits. The person testing us can stir our own angers and fears. All emotions are heightened, not just positive ones. The person I love can be the person for whom I feel intense hatred in such moments. The person with whom I am endlessly patient can equally make me vehemently angry. It can be frightening to find that we are capable of violence or rejection no less than that of the person we support, as this is the very opposite of how we wish to see ourselves as committed supporters.

The great gain of such moments is realising that we share the same humanity as the person we support. We all have our shadow side. The first step for the supporter is self-acceptance, not denying the darkness that has surfaced, not retreating into the pretence of being a 'whole' person who has chosen to work with 'broken' people. Our shared vulnerability can open a deeper empathy in us, helping us to understand and accept the other person better too.

Seeing it in this way also makes us aware of our own need to grow. We are asked to become aware of our contribution to the difficulties, realising that our impatience, inflexibility or lack of humour, could be a source of huge frustration for the person we are supporting. It is us who need to change if we are to learn to relieve such tensions and allow things to move on.

KEY QUESTIONS

Arising out of this recognition of common humanity, supporters therefore need to form a basic attitude of mind that asks *"If I was this person, what I would be feeling that would cause me to act the way I do; what message would I be giving through my behaviour?*

The focus needs to be on the emotional message and in trying to understand and dignify the person's needs and difficulties. This can be done in the following ways, as this story by Melanie's supporter illustrates.

Highlighting all that is good about the person.

Violence and aggression were pretty close to Melanie, but. I was not afraid of her and I began to like her. She also had gentleness, a caring in her, and a sense of humour. I felt that there was a beautiful person hidden inside, and we only got to see that part once in a while. At such moments I would march her to a mirror and say "Look, Melanie, here is this lovely person" and she could not even look at herself.

Availing of personal moments of nurturing.

Melanie was clingy, wanting to move too close to you. People feared something sexual in that and naturally tended to move away, sometimes in an offensive or dismissive manner. It seemed to me that she ached to be held, to be touched by somebody in a way that said, "I like you." She had no way of expressing that. But she also had to learn when and with whom physical contact was appropriate.

One day she saw her father get a massage for his sore back. She came to me and said, "My Dad has a sore back and I do too." I am leery about massaging anybody but that evening I said to her "Melanie, I don't think your back is sore, but I will give you a backrub because it feels nice." And I did, in a non-intimate, non-sexual sort of way. It was very simple but very therapeutic. Over the course of weeks it began to work. She seemed to lose the obsession to cling to people. She had needed to be touched in a gentle, respectful way that said 'I like you,' and when she got that she became more peaceful.

De-escalating and de-personalising tensions that arise.

Our goal is to seek to avoid conflict and minimising its importance where it does occur. The supporter must not take things personally, realising that difficulties are arising because the person does not know how else to deal with needs or fears. But it is not easy.

> I spent months trying to help Melanie with her anger; trying to teach her other ways of dealing with things rather than hitting people; trying to get to what was hurting her. Things came to a head between us when she got very angry at a function, and I sought to remove her. Melanie turned around and smacked me across the face. I was very shocked and angry. I could not believe what had happened.

> With hindsight, Melanie hitting me was probably the best things that could have happened to our relationship. That was how she expressed her anger, her anguish. Not necessarily with me, personally, but it was a testing. She had been threatening for so long, it was as if she had to go through with it on some occasion, to see if I still loved her afterwards and was still not afraid of her.

Showing a willingness to forgive.

Even people that care deeply for each other behave at times in ways that are damaging and unacceptable. That is why forgiveness is essential in all relationships. It is the fundamental attitude which says to the other person: "You are accepted, cared about, and believed in as you are, whatever your difficulties or weaknesses." Without forgiveness, a relationship becomes stuck and withers, leaving the person rejected and powerless.

> That evening, we had a long talk, and Melanie's pain was evident. We ended up crying together, me because she hurt me, and she because she hurt me, and both of us were probably touching into other pains from other years and other events, other relationships. So, it was two women forgiving one another and starting over fresh.

Respecting the other person's pace of growth.

> We tried to respect Melanie's time of growing. When working on her behaviour, we did not work on her eating or her socializing; we worked on just the violence. Other things we let go. And she did grow. It took three or four years, but she did it in her own time. Sometimes I want a person to grow faster than she does herself, and it does not work.

Offering appropriate love, affection, and security

This needs to be unconditional, so the person experiences being cared about regardless of his or her behaviour.

> No matter what happened, or how difficult things had been, I always tried to reassure Melanie afterwards that we cared about her. It was separating her behaviour from herself, trying to get the message across that we don't like what you are doing but we still like you. If things had been bad, I would try to spend some time with her in the evening, to put that day behind us and talk about tomorrow as a new start. Sometimes that worked, sometimes not, but slowly we managed to give her enough security, enough of a sense of being loved, that bit-by-bit she was changing. Other people began appreciating her more. They could see her sense of humour and her gentleness. They began to like her.

Arising from the experience of being treated in such a way, acceptance and trust grows. Often this happens quite easily, because of the openness and ease of both parties, but at times it is as complex and demanding as Melanie's story. Whether it happens easily or through great struggle, the ground is being laid for a deepening of the relationship.

STAGE FOUR: MUTUALITY AND INTERDEPENDENCE

Mutuality is the fourth stage of the deepening relationship: both people contribute to the relationship and both experience gain. There is a balance of giving and receiving by both parties. Where this is lacking, resentment from one or other person can set in, damaging their relationship.

Appreciating the other person's gifts

It is important that the supporter pays particular attention to what he or she receives from the relationship. There is always a gift to be recognized and appreciated, as Agnes found down through the years of her work.

> They have kept me mentally young and alert. They motivate me to learn new things that I can use with them. They have given me loads of fun and laughter. They taught me that the only way to be happy is to accept what you've got, limitations and all, and to accept yourself the way you are. They have also taught me to appreciate my freedom and to know how lucky I am.

True reciprocity means that each person is open to being changed and enhanced by the other. When a relationship is struggling, one person may think that matters will only improve if the other person changes, but in reality both parties need to change. The supporter is asked to give of him or herself for the sake of the other, but in a way that is good for both parties. Usually this is done in a simple, daily fashion, but sometimes what is happening goes deep not only for the person but also for the supporter.

> I was very conscious that I saw myself in Anne. The same questions she had with her parents, I had with mine. Her resentment and anger towards me, the parent figure, was how I had been with my mother. If I could help Anne come through that faster, not only would she stop causing me anguish, but in some ways, maybe I could live through her what I wish I had lived better with my mother. So in dealing with Anne, I was trying to deal with in myself at the same time, and that was hard. And yet, in spite of all the mistakes I made or maybe because of them, she has grown – a lot of good things did happen.

The discovery of one another

Many supporters create mutual relationships naturally. Others may be held back by a view of the carer-client professional relationship that makes the idea of reciprocity and interdependence quite threatening.

As noted earlier, it is a terrible form of death of the human spirit never to have one's gifts recognized or asked for. Some people know such a dying because mutuality has never been present. If a person does not have the experience of offering something that is valued by the supporter, it confirms low self-esteem and the associated fear of rejection. That is why the supporter has a major role in affirming a person's gifts – receiving them with gratitude and sharing them with others.

The most attractive settings for people to be in are the ones where good relationships are obvious and each person's presence and own capacity for caring is appreciated. Mutuality gives rise to security and closeness and creates the spaces where the individual finds a quality of life that is satisfying, not just because emotional needs are met, but because what the person has to offer is being asked for and appreciated.

STAGE FIVE: LOSS, CHANGE, AND ENDINGS

The final stage is inevitable – loss, change and endings are a reality for every person in relationships. Even life-long relationships have to end sometime. Although distress and loneliness are associated with parting, it is far better to have to deal with that than being denied the gift of the relationship in the first place. Few would say it would have been better if the relationship had never happened. Instead, we value the memories after the relationship has ended.

Because of fear that people could be hurt by a supporter's time-limited involvement in their lives, it is sometimes said that deep relationships between them should be avoided. The creation of unnecessary dependencies is certainly wrong, but were a supporter to remain emotionally aloof, the person gets a very damaging message. Perceived indifference hurts as much as more obvious forms of rejection. The person supported has the same right as everybody to know both the richness of relationship and the pain of loss, and to refuse the former for fear of the latter would be demeaning and patronising.

Preparing for loss

What matters is how loss, change or endings are handled and that they be planned for through the ordinary events of life[55]. Where an upcoming change is greater than just a temporary absence, people can be prepared. The meaning of the change should be discussed, even if one is uncertain how much the person understands. A farewell party both celebrates and acknowledges what has been, and allows the expression of loss.

It is valuable to teach a vulnerable person how to deal with someone being away, such as Joan used to do with Melanie.

> If Melanie knew I had to leave, whether it was a holiday, a meeting, whatever, she would be horrible the whole time I was gone and get back at me on my return. So I began to prepare her. We talked about how long I was going for and marked it on her calendar. We marked when I was coming back – a happy face – and talked about how she did not need to act out, and that I understood it was hard for her when I was not there.

Learning to deal with temporary absences also prepared Melanie for Joan's ultimate departure from being her paid supporter.

> I kept stressing that my going away had nothing to do with her. I said I knew that we were going to miss each other, but that we would see each other when I got back. We would plan things weeks ahead so that we had something to look forward to. I worked hard to make sure there was no sense of being abandoned.

The coming and going of paid supporters is the cause of difficulty for many people. It is only one of many reasons why it is important that the person be part of a network of relationships far beyond the service setting, so that the loss of a valued supporter does not leave the individual in an emotional or social void.

It is also part of humanity that all relationships don't get better, that some relationships sever. It is not always possible to work out situations that are unhappy, no matter how much this is wished for.

The ending of an unhappy relationship can also be a new beginning. It can bring somebody who is able to connect with a person that others were not able to reach. Someone new can bring a new sensitivity, a new approach – the possibility of new life and new relationships.

As happens in most people's lives when an important figure moves away, efforts should be made to maintain contact afterwards. For example, there could be visits, maybe for a meal, or an occasional card or phone call can mean a great deal.

Death: the final loss

Hopefully the day is past when it was considered proper to protect the people from the reality and pain of death. Not infrequently funerals were not attended, and it could be weeks before a person learned of the death of a close relation. Services failed in their duty by not finding out what people themselves wanted and supporting that. Conspiracy and deceit often led to confusion and a loss of trust[56].

In fact, the person being 'protected' has often experienced so many separations already. They are the ones who can help others accept death, as seen in May's story.

> John had developed Alzheimer's disease and it was obvious that death was approaching. May was a frail lady who cried easily. John was her "big honey" and she was distressed at the thought of his death. She visited regularly and prayed for him every night.

> The question was whether the service would be able to support John in his last weeks, or should he go to a nursing home? Views were mixed, and May was a particular concern. She was so vulnerable and so close to John, people feared the upset would kill her.

> Despite such fears, it was decided to set things up so that John could stay at home to die. As the end approached, May was not frightened. She continued to visit every day and would say, as always, "Oh my big honey! Give my big honey a kiss!"

> And when John died, May came over to see him. Her eyes streamed with tears, but she was not in pieces, not broken in depression. She was just May, like she always had been. She said "John is gone. I can't see John any more. But John is in here now" – pointing to her heart. She knew exactly, no question. She could not see him anymore, but he was right there, close as ever. Those who had supported John to the end were profoundly moved and felt that the decision to care for him at home had been fully validated by the simple beauty and depth of May's response to his death.

The person who needs support in living has the right to experience life in its fullness, to know times sad as well as happy, to celebrate what has been good in a relationship, and to mourn its passing when that time comes. A true relationship is emotionally honest.

THE SAME STAGES BUT MAYBE NOT THE SAME INTENSITY

In this chapter we have looked at the process of relationship development, using stories that may seem extreme in the difficulties that were encountered. The value of these true stories is the way in which they highlight the complexity of what may happen for both the person and the supporter as a relationship evolves. All human relationships have similar stages of development, but maybe not the same intensity. The supporter's awareness may be even more important in the case of quieter individuals whose needs may not be recognised because they do not cause a fuss. It is also important to have knowledge of relationship development when encouraging and supporting wider friendships, as described in the following chapter.

FRIENDSHIPS AND INTIMACY

I get by with a little help from my friends. **John Lennon**

Modern society has more lonely people than ever before and the people we support are not immune to this trend. What is remarkable both in mainstream society and in disability services is the assumption that friendships are an optional extra; a bonus if you have them but you can still get by if you don't!

Yet it need not be so. One of the ignored roles that support staff must play in services is encouraging friendships for the people they support. There are many possibilities for doing this among their peers, family members and the wider community.

Our focus here is still on building relationships between two people. In later chapters we will explore relationships within communities. We do not mean to imply that friendships between two people have to be divorced from a wider circle of friends and acquaintances. Everybody needs both. But people may still need support to develop friendships from among those with whom they are acquainted.

Also a word of caution: people may not need or want our help when it comes to developing friendships. We have to beware of interfering in their personal lives. As always, we need to be invited to help and cautious about directing their choice of friendships.

Preferring NOT to have friends

We should also consider the possibility that some people have no interest in having friends and therefore there is no need to find friends for them! We have certainly heard this view stated by parents – mostly older ones, but not exclusively so – as well as by support staff at review meetings. They point out that the person is happy to stay at home, or that they prefer to be alone, or else they explain how agitated they become when they meet new people or when they are taken to new settings. We don't doubt that preferring to be alone can happen just as some non-disabled people make similar choices. But we would question whether or not a lack of interest in having friends is a genuine choice or an unchallenged habit? And even if it was their choice, is it necessarily a good one for them to make?

DEVELOPING ACQUAINTANCES

At the outset four basic truths about friendship have to be stated[57].

- We cannot make friendships for other people; people choose their own friends. At best we can help them to build up a network of acquaintances out of which friendships may develop.

- Friendships usually grow out of shared interests and activities and from among people already known to each other. It can be easier to rekindle old friendships rather than to create totally new ones.

- Physical appearance is often what initially draws us to people. Likewise odd behaviours or unusual appearances may cause people to shy away. We need to encourage the people we support to dress fashionably and look their best. We need to provide opportunities so that people's personality can shine through.

- Friendships are based around mutual choice and self-determination. Hence we need to constantly consult and listen to the people we are trying to help. We must not impose *our* values and preferences on to another person.

Friendships often seem to happen or emerge, almost by chance. But that is not so as the points above illustrate. It is possible to steer people towards friendships and to nurture them. Below, we explore three approaches that have been successful in creating acquaintances that can lead to friendships.

1. We first consider the need for support staff to take on the role of 'go-betweens' in making introductions and building acquaintances.

2. We examine what's entailed in supporting people with their friendships.

3. We move on to look at the idea of recruiting people specifically to be-friend an individual person.

These approaches may not be needed with everyone. If provided with oppor-tunities to be in the company of others, people will create their own acquaintances and friendships. This can happen in all spheres of life and we will provide many examples in the next chapters of the book. But even then, supporters can still have an important role to play in putting people in touch with one another and helping to sustain emerging friendships.

THE NEED FOR GO-BETWEENS

As the name implies, a 'go-between' is somebody who is connected to two people who do not know each other until they are introduced. The go-between usually takes their lead from one of the parties and acts on his or her behalf. For example, supporters know the needs, interests and talents of the people they support and through their connections in the neighbourhood or with various community groups, they are able to bring people together. Hence the first requirement for a go-between is to be able to identify community connections that could be possibly made with individuals or groups in their area.

The second requirement of a go-between is being prepared to ask people to get involved. David Schwartz[58] identified asking as one of the most crucial weapons in the armoury of social connectors. He noted the reluctance there can be on the part of professional staff and carers to ask favours of others because it goes against various social conventions and may even threaten our own self-image (see box).

The third crucial role for 'go-betweens' is making introductions. Like a good host or hostess, the 'go-between' needs to put the strangers at their ease with one another. This means facilitating conversation, finding joint activities for them to do and when the opportunity arises, discretely withdrawing for a time so that the two people can get on with one another.

> **Why are people afraid of asking?**
>
> - Perhaps because they are afraid of being rejected: the people they ask may say "no". Yet most people are disposed to help and very few would ever be rude and critical.
>
> - Perhaps because families or services have such high expectations of potential friends, they cannot find people who meet their standards.
>
> - Perhaps they fear that the potential friend will feel there is nothing in it for them, that there are no benefits to helping a person in need of support. However as we saw in Chapter 1 there is much to be gained from friendships with those we support.

Finally, the 'go-between' needs to be supportive of the blooming partnership by keeping in touch with both parties; checking how things are going; making discrete suggestions and subtly praising them for how well they are getting on with each other!

The contribution of such 'go-betweens' in the lives of people with disabilities has been best captured in the work of Robert Edgerton[59]. He described the crucial role of people he termed 'benefactors' in helping people with intellectual disabilities discharged from long-stay hospitals to socially integrate into local communities. However this dependence decreased over time as people merged into society and some even went on to become benefactors to other non-disabled members in their neighbourhood.

Rarely are these people-linking tasks written into the job descriptions of professional workers nor are people recruited for their people-connecting skills. Yet most of us have acquired these skills and we utilise them in our personal lives so perhaps their use with the people we support could be readily encouraged, if only this was recognised at a priority.

Finally, in modern society there are other avenues opening up for people to enlist the services of various types of 'go-betweens' to help them. These include Internet chat-rooms, single clubs and dating agencies. None of these options have been designed with the specific needs and vulnerabilities of the people we support in mind and each could present particular dangers to them. However the concepts underlying these agencies might be used to develop similar and safer opportunities. Some disability organisations internationally offer these functions to their members and perhaps these new types of services will come to the fore in future years[60].

SUPPORTING ACQUAINTANCES

In human society, being acquainted with others is a sign of acceptance and inclusion. You have other people to talk to, who will acknowledge you, ask after you and generally look out for you. Supporters may have to help people build up a network of acquaintances by introducing them to others, such as neighbours, and assisting with the small talk that helps to build the relationship.

Some acquaintances will blossom into friendships of their own accord but when this does not happen a helping hand might be called-for. An often ignored location for furthering acquaintances is the person's home.

Home Entertainment

Inviting others for a coffee, a barbeque, a meal, a party or even just to watch a video together provides an opportunity for people to get to know one another better. The hosting skills of the supporter really come to the fore here in creating a warm welcome for visitors. As well as helping visitors to relax and settle, their goal is to support the person in fulfilling the 'hosting role' with their guest. Home settings allow everyone the chance to meet with others; even those who may be largely housebound because of their disabilities.

Invitations to visit may lead to return invites to people's homes be they family, peers or people in the locality. Again the persons may depend on a supporter to encourage or to accompany them, but once settled they can discretely withdraw and arrange a time to call back.

Marjorie had lived away from her family for over 20 years. Her sisters lived many miles away but kept in touch mostly by telephone. They would drop in from time-to-time if they were in the vicinity and they sent photographs of their children which Marjorie proudly displayed in her bedroom. One day an invitation came for Marjorie to attend the wedding of her nephew. She was thrilled and obviously wanted to go but her support staff didn't think it was possible. How would she get there? Who would look after her? The family weren't offering to help. At the next staff meeting, the talk was about holidays. Then Marjorie's key-worker had a brain-wave – why don't they combine the wedding with a holiday for Marjorie and her friends. A B&B was booked for three nights! Marjorie was dropped off at her sister's house on the day of the wedding while the others went to the beach. She really enjoyed herself. For many of the family it was chance to meet Marjorie for the first time. Now she has regular invitations to family gatherings and stays over occasionally.

As friendships develop, people could be invited to stay overnight or for a weekend, if there's room in the house. Of course this may mean extra work and responsibilities for family carers (if the person still lives at home) or for paid supporters in services. Maybe this is one of the reasons why these opportunities rarely happen for people we support but the consequence is that the person is denied the chance to form friendships and in a way that we have all experienced in our own lives.

Mutual support

We also need to promote people as sources of support to others and not just receivers of support. It is the mutuality of support that each gets from, and gives to, the other, that is a hallmark of friendships. This is the basis around which many advocacy groups function but it must feature in all relationships if they are to grow into friendships. Hence support staff may need to find opportunities for people to become supporters of others, and encourage them to take on this role. This can take various forms; from practical assistance to providing a sympathetic ear.

Key Ring[61] is a housing provider for people with learning disabilities that works by building up mutually supportive networks among the tenants living within a geographical area as well as linking them into the communities where they live. Tenants are encouraged to contact one another if they need assistance: a light bulb changed; their grass cut; a cake baked or a lift to the shops. Support staff are still available but they too are part of a mutual support Ring; helping each other out when asked, or offering when they see a person needs help.

Similarly people with disabilities can make significant contributions to community life: fetching newspapers for housebound neighbours; greeting people as they come to church; making tea at the Bingo sessions and so on. They can become volunteer helpers at lunch clubs, charity shops and dog kennels. In all these ways, new images are created of people with disabilities as competent, contributing citizens. This is a vital and much neglected aspect of building networks of acquaintances and of helping to create a sense of community. This is a theme we will develop in Chapter 7 of the book.

Support staff can make it happen as long as they are willing to see themselves as part of a wider community and not just a staff member in a care service. This may mean searching out opportunities for people to participate in educational, leisure or work activities that will enable them to become acquainted with other people; be they family, peers or others in the neighbourhood.

Developing social skills

Some people may lack the social skills required to make and keep relationships. For example, their behaviour or communication is perhaps off-putting. Supporters may need to make clear to person the impact they are having on other people and show how he or she might act differently. This could be done through one-to-one reviews or within a small group that comes together to focus on social skills training[62].

> I had a row with my girlfriend. The staff said I should buy her a box of chocolates and say sorry. But it was her fault. She should say sorry to me. I need my money – she has more money than me and never buys me anything. I do lose my temper I know, but she started it. She's coming to tea next week and Mark (key-worker) says we could have a chat with her then- the three of us. That's OK by me but I'm not buying any chocolates – no way.

Equally supporters may have to provide potential acquaintances or friends with feedback about the value of the relationship if the person they have befriended is unable to do so or resists doing it. There's a sense in which the new friends also need social and emotional support to help sustain the relationship especially in the early stages or when it hits a rocky patch. Even a short telephone call to check how things are going can be very much appreciated.

> I've known Mary for years and when she got a support worker's job she invited me to one of the socials they organised. That's where I first met Joan – a strange lady and that's putting it mildly! However she seemed to take a shine on me and she sat close by me although never looked me in the eye. Mary telephoned about a week later and said Joan keeps asking about me – would I come to see her? I went along and she practically ignored me but when I was about to go, she brought in her photo album. We looked at it together and then suddenly she's out of the chair and off to her room. A few days later, I saw Mary at Tesco's and she said Joan had started talking about her new friend – me! I volunteered to call round again and it soon became a habit. We take turns to go to each house on Tuesday nights. That's how I came to know Joan and now we've become good friends. It's helped make up for losing my husband.

RECRUITING BE-FRIENDERS

Some people because of the nature of their difficulties will find it hard to make and keep acquaintances. We need then to find people who are willing to be-friend such individuals and who will tolerate – at least for a time – a different kind of friendly relationship; one in which they may put in some extra effort to sustain the friendship. They are probably not a friend in the full sense of the word so a variety of words are used to describe them: *befrienders, buddies, mentors; advocates*[63]. At the heart of all these concepts is a relationship between one person and someone from outside the support services. In time, these may become mutual friendships but this is not presumed at the outset.

> Jo had taken early retirement from working in a day centre for people with learning disabilities. The social worker attached to the centre, approached her about taking part in a family breaks scheme that was starting in the area as respite for elderly carers. Over a period of weeks Jo would be matched with an individual who needed a break. He or she would come to stay in Jo's home for some hours on a Saturday or Sunday but through time this could build up into overnight stays. Jo would be re-imbursed for her expenses and throughout the social worker would maintain contact and provide support.

With some reluctance Jo agreed to give it a try. Although it wasn't easy at first and she thought of giving up after some disastrous visits, she's now been doing it for four years. She says: "I love having Nancy to stay – I am so fond of her, she reminds me of my Mother and that's probably why. You become so very attached to them, they become part of the family, part of the furniture and you look forward to them coming as much as they look forward to it".

Schemes of this sort give us some clues as to how befrienders can be recruited and retained.

Word of mouth: People are more likely to respond to a personal request than a newspaper advert or radio appeal. This can mean asking among your own friends and acquaintances, or asking other work colleagues to pass on the request to their contacts. This approach has the added advantage that people can be given more details about what is expected of them and it reduces the risk of undesirable people becoming involved (but does not eliminate it!).

Target suitable people: A positive response is often more forthcoming from certain groups. These include: people who have experience of working in services or who have previously volunteered; family members of persons with a learning disability; students interested in a career in social services; church groups and those enrolled with voluntary services. Even so, all prospective friends will have to be police-checked and interviewed by a selection panel appointed to vet applications. This is to safeguard people from abuse.

Matching on interests: It helps if people have some shared interests – be it sitting at home watching the television, gardening, watching football matches or hill walking. This should not prevent people from trying new things but often it is easier to begin with familiar activities.

Gradual introduction: People need time to get to know on another. People may first meet as part of a larger group; then spend a short time alone together before moving on to longer visits. Incidentally potential befrienders may feel more at ease if this happens in places with which they are familiar rather than in service settings where they are strangers.

Named contact person: Having the name and telephone number of a person they can contact at any time is a necessary support for new befrienders. They may never use it but it is always a reassurance to them. Likewise a follow-up phone call following a visit is also appreciated and gives you a chance to confirm if things went well.

Payment for expenses: The delicate subject of expenses needs to be discussed with the befriender; for example some services will cover the travel costs of befrienders or their admission to events when the accompany the person. Voluntary group fund-raise for these activities or else they come from the person's social security benefits. However these payments may actually get in the way of a real friendship developing.

Planned withdrawal: Friendships don't always last for ever and so it can be with befriending. There may come a time when befrienders have to move on; just as service staff leave their jobs. If a parting has to happen, explain the reasons for it and if possible plan carefully how it comes about.

Some cautions

Recruiting specific befrienders for a person is not an ideal solution. There are some cautions we should note.

- The matching of 'friends' is often done by a professional worker or scheme coordinator; hence the person with learning disabilities has very limited scope for choosing and developing their own friendships.
- The 'friendship' that develops runs the risk of being artificial in the sense that the friend is invariably cast in the role of helper and supervisor. Through time this can place quite a strain on the relationship if the person's demands are high.
- The motives of the two parties for entering these schemes can be very different. One may come wanting to do voluntary work, to gain work experience or 'to give back something', while the other is there because they are lonely, bored and depressed, and maybe the doctor or social workers has referred them! In some ways, volunteer friends who are paid expenses cannot be real friends in just the same way staff are not.
- The 'find-a-friend' approach is an example of adopting a specialist solution to a disability issue – "let's create a new type of professional!" Therein lies the risk that busy supporters will no longer nurture friendships as part of their role because now the person has a nominated friend.
- Some paid supporters, and family members in particular, might be wary of befrienders being encouraged with a member of the opposite sex. The challenge is to persuade more males to become befrienders.

Even with these cautions, befriending schemes have resulted in some rich and enduring relationships that otherwise would never have happened.

BARRIERS TO FRIENDSHIPS

It can be quite a struggle to nurture friendships. Knowing the barriers that people face may start you thinking about how they can be overcome should they arise for the people you support. Here are some commonly experienced barriers.

Independent travel: When people are dependent on others to take them by car or accompany them on public transport, their freedom to meet up with their friends is much curtailed. Could the person learn to travel independently? There are certainly various training packages now available for doing this.

Lack of money: It can be costly to pay for travel and entertainment. Are there ways people might share costs or find less costly alternatives?

The attitudes of people in the community: Old stereotypes and prejudices prevent people making any effort to get to know people whom they see as being very different to themselves. Hence the emphasis we have placed on making introductions and giving people the opportunity to meet in relaxed surroundings.

Fears regarding sexual expression: Family members and some paid supporters may be fearful of a sexual dimension emerging in friendships, particularly with members of the opposite sex.

Positive identity: If people lack self-confidence and have a poor opinion of themselves, then they are less likely to make an effort to meet others. Belonging to a self-advocacy group has helped to increase people's self-respect as well as providing opportunities for friendships to develop.

Losing touch: People can lose touch with their friends once they leave school or college, move house or change jobs. Can we help people to keep in touch by phone or email, by visits to each other homes or by sharing activities?

Many things can conspire to make people lonely. It does require a determined effort to create opportunities for friendships. To our thinking this is one of the most neglected roles of supporters.

BECOMING AND REMAINING FRIENDS

The transition from acquaintances to friendships happens in many different ways and can take place naturally without much conscious effort. Nonetheless support staff have an ongoing role to play in helping this process and in sustaining friendships.

Friends need opportunities to keep in touch one another, preferably face-to-face or by telephone. People need to meet their friends in a range of settings outside of the home. Often these are based around a shared activity that brings people together (see Chapter 6). However certain activities are better than others in nurturing friendships. Here are some ways for judging them.

- Are people meeting in relaxed and enjoyable situations?
- Can people participate equally in the activity without too much help and assistance?
- Are there opportunities for people to 'pair-off' during the activity so that they can get to know one another more personally?
- If desired, can people have some private times together?
- Are there opportunities for people to share their feelings, opinions and beliefs? This will help to deepen the relationship.

Some of the time-honoured means of meeting and mixing with people fulfil these requirements: dances, music making, walks, sports, bingo, cooking and craft activities. Of course some of the features highlighted can still be incorporated into many other activities that are not particularly social such as watching television and listening to music!

Once again, the clue in deciding which activities to suggest is to take your lead from the person's interest. It may require some detective work to find out what is happening in the locality and maybe a little nerve to go along to them for the first time.

Supporters may have a particularly significant role to play with people who have communication difficulties. As we noted in a previous chapter, it is possible to overcome these difficulties but new persons may struggle at first. It helps having an experienced communicator who can 'interpret' a person's communications for others. This also gives them an example as to how they might adjust their communications. Passing on advice and practical tips can be a vital support to both parties as they get to know one another.

As people become more comfortable with one another, the supporters can gradually withdraw. This is a fine judgment to make: do it too soon and the budding friendship may falter; stay too long and you get in the way of a friendship ever developing.

Martin and Jane were in the special care section in the day centre they attended. Both had limited verbal communication and required help with most of their personal care needs. At the weekly Disco, Martin and Jane invariably partnered one another; having eyes for no one else. When they thought no one was looking, they sneaked a hug or two! When staff realised how much the friendship meant to them both, they gave them the chance to have lunch together at the centre and apart from the other people in their groups.

They lived in different group homes, some ten miles apart but every other week, Martin would go back with Jane to her house for the evening meal and likewise Jane went to Martin's. Often they were content to simply be in each other's company because barely a word passed between them but plenty of smiles were exchanged as they watched a video or listened to music.

We probably know least about how to sustain friendships over time. Undoubtedly there are many examples of life-long friendships but we have an imperfect understanding of why this happens for some and not for others. Then again, change is a feature of everyone's friendships and sometimes this can be good for all concerned.

However supporting long-term friendships is particularly challenging for services as many of the front-line staff they employ have high turnover rates. New staff may not be aware of the history of relationships in the lives of the people they support; how they came about, of the personalities involved in them and their shared experiences. They may fail to appreciate the contribution that these friendships have made, and continue to make to the person's well being.

Thus we venture to suggest, that just as a new girl-friend or boyfriend needs to get to know their partner's wider circle of friends and families, so too new support staff need to make a point of getting to know the people in the social networks of the people they support. This will at least provide some insight into the history of their friendships.

It will also make it easier for them to act as a 'go-between' if misunderstandings, disputes or fall-outs arise between the two parties. They can deploy their social support skills through helping to repair communication breakdowns or encourage the formation of new acquaintances and networks; all of the things we have discussed previously. In a sense, building friendships always has to be ongoing because the nature of life is that people constantly fall into and out of relationships.

INTIMATE RELATIONSHIPS

Just as friendships grow out of our acquaintances, so in turn, friendships can develop into more intimate relationships. This is part of our humanity and cannot be denied to the people we support. Hence in this final section we explore the responsibilities involved in supporting people to find and sustain intimate relationships. These relationships can arise between opposite or same sex couples.

Sometimes these can be short-lived infatuations but many yearn for a more committed relationship that can last over many years and may lead to people deciding to live together and to get married. Such relationships play a vital part in people's lives and may be the only constant amidst the turnover in service staff and befrienders.

My name is Richard, I'm Pam's boyfriend and we've been together ten years and two months. We met when I was on holiday in Wexford. We were just friends then. Later we met up again in Clonmel. I came back there for respite; I wasn't well and stayed for nine months. One afternoon just before supper I took Pam out in the car park there was only the two of us. I said, "You know Pam I missed you an awful lot, I missed you an awful lot for years and I like you … I love you much".

Later in my sister's son's house, Pam and him were looking at engagement rings in a book. And I said, "I'll tell you what Pam we'll get engaged, why not? We, we love each other". I spread the word around everyplace that we were getting engaged. I gave many speeches that we were getting engaged.

We had a massive big engagement party. There was tea, coffee, scones, cake and everything. And there was a big crowd. And there was two chairs, one for me and one for Pam, and we were sitting down in chairs, and the priest came up and got the rings and, and put the rings on our fingers. And we got engaged and, we very, very happy. And we are engaged four years and three months already. We've our own wee house that Pam keeps clean and I do the garden. We go places; we enjoy each other's company. We have an odd fight, but I know Pam, and she's a very, very nice young attractive good-looking girl. I do love Pam very, very much; I'd do anything for her.

We admit though, that not everyone feels that sexual intimacy is desirable for people who have intellectual disabilities or who are otherwise vulnerable[64].

- Some think of them as 'eternal children' or holy innocents' and feel that sexuality is of no interest to them or that it will unsettle them if the issue is brought into the open.

- Others maintain that they are unable to guard themselves against exploitation and hurt. Nor do they understand the responsibilities that come with intimate relationships. Hence it is better not to encourage relationships and to raise unrealistic expectations.

- For some people, the issue is linked with morality. They may feel sex outside of marriage is wrong, as is the use of birth control. Same sex attraction and relationships are also frowned on. The only option they advocate is celibacy.

- It is thought that women in particular may be exploited sexually by their male partners who are often focussed on satisfying their own desires rather than creating a mutually enjoyable relationship[65]. This can be avoided by preventing sexual activity taking place.

But these deeply held beliefs have to be set against other facts.

- The people we support have sexual feelings. It is part of nearly everyone's biological make-up.

- Many are curious about sexual matters which in modern society are commonly mentioned on television and radio programmes at all times of the day.

- They are vulnerable to sexual abuse if the issue is ignored. People need to be taught about their sexual and emotional development so that they can appreciate when abuse is occurring or know the words to tell others what happened to them.

- If they seek it, they are entitled to the pleasure and satisfaction that comes from physical intimacy that is enjoyable and life affirming rather than harmful.

- People can be content with different degrees of intimacy. Some are content to hold hands or cuddle and kiss and have no desire for sexual intercourse. Fear of the latter should not preclude other forms of sensual and emotional intimacy.

At its most basic though, it's an issue of equal rights. We cannot say that the people we support have the right to equality of housing, employment and health but draw a line around their sexuality. For too long, families and services ignored the issue of sex and relationships. Thankfully most services have developed policies to guide paid supporters in their responses[66]. Increasingly training courses are available also for support staff and sometimes for family members. There are information packages specifically for people with learning difficulties[67]. Yet an unspoken edict still pervades in many places that sexuality is a risky topic and one that is best avoided[68].

SUPPORTING INTIMACY

Admittedly we still have much to learn about how best to support people in intimate relationships but there are some pointers that will not let us down.

- Relationships must be the choice of the persons involved.
- Supporters must respect the person's choice of partner and help them to enjoy and develop their friendship.
- Supporters have to treat them as a couple when it comes to planning activities that they can do together or which will bring them together.
- The couple will need times and opportunities for privacy.

All in all, we should take pleasure in the benefits that the friendship brings to the couple, while being watchful of the risks that can arise.

Equally supporters may need to help the couple work through the problems or difficulties that such a relationship may encounter from time-to-time. There is a higher risk of this occurring among people who have been starved of relationships. The high emotional investment they place in the friendship can put particular pressure on the relationship. In particular, they may need assistance with the 'negotiation' skills needed to repair disputes and disagreements, such as trying to see the other's viewpoint, being prepared to listen to their hurt, apologising for actions done in haste, and finding ways of showing respect and love for their partner.

People who chose to live together or to get married will present a fresh set of challenges to services for which many are unprepared. In these instances, 'couple-centred' planning and support is required rather than person-centred planning especially around their understanding of sex and sexual health, marriage and cohabiting, and the commitments required of one another. They will need particular support in coming to decisions about having children. Specialist advice should be sought, as this is a complex issue.

However all supporters may be called on to give advice and support, such as Marjorie.

This is an area of work I feel very committed to: I hate to think the people I support are unnecessarily deprived of the benefits of friendships and intimate relationships. I found to provide this support you have to have a relationship with the couple, you can't come at it cold. It feels totally wrong to me to sit down and have meetings about these issues with a person or couple, that involve a number of other people (and their parents, heaven forbid!). I certainly wouldn't accept a situation like that for myself.

With Joe and Elizabeth, we started talking at a weekend away while doing outdoor pursuits. Now I usually talk to Joe whilst working alongside him, perhaps at the kitchen sink. Making eye contact and sitting down facing each other is too intimidating and embarrassing for him. Over a period of four years we've reached the position where they have married and are now expecting their first child. But it's been a long haul and will continue on into the future. Both have benefited from pre-marriage counselling with a psychologist who often works with people with learning disabilities. And they continued counselling after marriage, both separately and together.

With both Joe and Mary I've had to be very aware of the language I use; I've had to keep things clear and simple and use the appropriate slang on occasion. Pictures were not necessary but I know they can be helpful in some situations.

Working towards independence has also been a challenge. Financial issues (which are difficult for many couples) have emerged. Mary says: "how can I buy food when he has spent all the food money on videos?" Joe says: "She's no fun any more, she wants to spend all our money on baby clothes".

It's also been very important for me not to feel left alone in this work but having a colleague I can talk to in confidence, not necessarily a supervisor, but someone who is working with similar issues and understands the need for confidentiality.

By contrast, people may come to a realisation that the relationship has run its course. That is their decision to make and rather than questioning the rights and wrongs of it, it's better to help them identify the reasons why they have come to that decision. They may also need help to deal with the emotional hurt if their partner ended a relationship that they wanted to continue.

In sum, you may need to provide the same sort of emotional support and guidance that you have given to your family and friends when they have encountered relationship problems. However, we stress that supporters also need to be aware of their limitations in this complex area of evolving practice. There may come a point when it is necessary to encourage the couple to seek help from other sources, such as specialists in relationship counselling.

CHALLENGES AND DILEMMAS

Undoubtedly, intimate relationships bring particular challenges and dilemmas for paid supporters and family carers as they struggle to accommodate it alongside their 'duty to care' responsibilities[69]. However many similar challenges are commonly encountered with other groups in society such as teenagers.

We have framed these challenges as a series of questions to which you may already know the answers but if you don't, you need to work with your co-supporters and managers in finding answers. Team working is essential in harnessing the wisdom and experience of all supporters. You do the people you support no favours by going-it-alone.

Have the couple received sex education? Are they aware of contraceptives? If the answer is no to one or both questions, then whose responsibility is it to ensure this happens? Who's available to provide this information?

Have they been taught to trust their own feelings? If they are feeling uncomfortable, do they know to look for help and advice?

Are the couple able to give meaningful consent? In the past people with 'mental impairments' were considered incapable of giving informed consent. Others had to make decisions for them. However the legal position is changing and there is growing appreciation that a person's capacity to consent has to be judged for each particular situation. This will centre around their understanding of both the nature and consequences of an act and whether they can agree freely to participate. Judgements about a person's capacity to consent should not be taken by an individual supporter. Rather this is best done by a group of people coming to an agreed decision; who must also document the reasons for it. Chapter 9 explores the issue of managing risk in greater detail.

Are the couple having a fling? Sexual activity between couples need not imply a lasting emotional relationship. This is sometimes referred to as 'casual sex' and modern society offers people many opportunities for it. Some would argue that people with learning disabilities have the same rights to partake in such relationships as their peers. But given the degree of supervision these people experience in their lives, it is unlikely to happen without some-one 'turning a blind eye'. Can paid staff afford to do this without the backing of their superiors? Is this likely to be forthcoming?

Does the relationship offend your morals or those of other supporters? Some supporters may not want to condone physical relationships between people of the same sex, or outside of marriage. This is an issue that supporters must share honestly with one another and all come to an agreed course of action. To do otherwise is to risk harming the relationship with the persons in need of support and with your colleagues.

Judy and Elsie had been in the same group home for three years but had been friends from their days in a special school. Much of their time was spent in each other's company; going to the cinema, social clubs and church. People thought they were twins as they both looked alike and behaved alike.

Support staff came to their house primarily to assist two other tenants. One morning a new member of staff arrived early at the house and after knocking went into Elsie's bedroom and to her surprise found Judy sleeping beside her rather than in her own bedroom. Elsie – clutching the bedclothes to cover her nakedness – looked embarrassed; maybe even guilty and started to make excuses. Judy just slept on!

This incident and others like it, raises a moral dilemma for the individual supporter. To whom are they responsible? Does she apologise to Elsie and Judy and respect their privacy by keeping it a secret? Or does she have to report what she saw to her line managers? Or should she discuss it with the two women and seek their advice?

Could the relationship be abusive or is it in danger of becoming so? This can include financial, emotional, physical as well as sexual abuse. You need to *sensitively* check out your suspicions; record them *factually* and be especially vigilant for any signs that are indicative of abuse.

Do individuals know who to talk to if bad things are happening in their relationship? Can they recognise and cope with bullying? Supporters need to signal their availability to discuss such matters.

These various challenges and dilemmas will continue to reverberate in our services for many years to come. Meantime it is helpful if:

– It is made clear by the service that paid supporters have responsibilities to provide non-judgemental support for intimate relationships chosen by the people they support.

– Clear guidelines are prepared for supporters that deal with the various questions noted above. These should be developed in association with the people you support.

– Time is given over at team meetings to discuss the implementation of the guidelines.

– Service mangers use one-to-one sessions to assist individual support staff to think through how they deal with the issues of concern.

– People in need of support are actively taught assertiveness and self-protection skills so that there is less danger of exploitation and abuse.

– People have a circle of support that will look out for them as well as assist them in their relationships.

– Supporters are watchful for signs of difficulties or distress that may be arising in intimate relationships.

Finally the topic of intimacy is just as applicable for people with severe and profound disabilities. For them, sexual intimacy may not arise but this should not preclude opportunities for physical contact through affectionate touching, cuddling and hand-holding. For example, they may need our help to be moved physically next to their friends and out of their wheelchairs.

LAST WORDS

The essential message of this chapter is that relationships enrich our lives. We need to look beyond service staff and family members in order to help the people to make friends with others such as their peers or the people they live or work alongside. This may take time and serious effort, and will require ongoing support that in itself will only be possible if it is built on trusted relationships. Fortunately, as the next two chapters of the book explain, supporters need not face these challenges alone.

BRINGING PEOPLE TOGETHER

Community is a place of belonging, where people find their identity.

Jean Vanier

We have looked at the crucial importance of relationships in peoples' lives, but these do not just mean one-to-one bonds. Relationships develop and are lived out within networks that link us in a mutually supportive and committed manner. That is what community means. Growing up, most of us experience this in our families. Later we belong to communities beyond the family – groups of friends, workers, club mates, or whatever.

This may not be the case for many of the people we support. They may not experience the same opportunities to play with other children around their homes and neighbourhood, to join in sports and youth activities, or to form acquaintances through leisure, education or work. Too often they live on the margins of society, excluded from community life.

SOCIAL ISOLATION

Social isolation is not restricted to those we support. Today there appears to be a greater emphasis on individualism and personal achievement, a diminished sense of responsibility for the common good and more isolated forms of entertainment, such as television. The result is more social isolation, leaving many people with an unfilled hunger for community.

During the World Games in Ireland, the athletes showed that if given half a chance, they could help to build that sense of community that is often lacking. Their humanity, spontaneity, gifts and needs drew people together when they stayed in towns and villages around the country. Despite barriers of language and culture, a powerful sense of community was created during those days. The athletes sparked overflowing generosity and celebration among their hosts.

Unfortunately those we support are seldom given the chance to be community builders. A focus on their limits and needs rather than on what they offer causes people to move away rather than to include them in their lives. Difficulties in communicating and in forming relationships can further reduce their chances of building spontaneous community networks. At times they are actively excluded and discriminated against. Many are integrated physically but not socially[70].

SUPPORTERS' COMMITMENT TO INCLUSIVITY

For these reasons, those we support need help in forming the links and bonds that would enrich their own and others' lives. This is so important that helping people find their place in their own communities should be a primary objective of supporters, whether family, friends, voluntary organisations or services.

The aim of fostering relationships and communities is explicit in many services' mission statement, but limited success to date begs the question as to how committed they are to doing so[71]? Power and influence is concentrated in the hands of managers and specialists, with the risk of diminishing the people we support and undermining informal networks, leaving untrained supporters feeling inadequate or on the margins. A shift of mind-set is required so that resources are re-allocated to what people themselves see as most important in their lives.

Turning words into reality also needs commitment by each service supporter. Person-centred plans are based on people's ambitions, identifying who will facilitate them in becoming involved in the way they wish. Ideally any funding issues are dealt with in the plan and a timescale for implementing specific steps is established[72].

But building social networks cannot be left only to the individual's supporter, who may have a lot of daily care needs to address. There is generally little time left for these supporters to seek out new social opportunities. Hence services have begun to employ personnel whose role is to assist in the building of truly inclusive communities, through engaging with local networks and organisations, by recruiting people as volunteers, and helping to create events and occasions that will enhance the experience of everybody involved, not just those needing support. This involves focussing on two basic ways in which networks of relationship come about:

- A sense of community grows among people because they share the same house, parish, town or region. Bonds form where people meet regularly – at the shops, collecting children at the school, attending local sport events; in places of work; in pubs, clubs, places of worship or where-ever. A major reason to support people to live in the area where they grew up is that they already have a sense of belonging, know the local people, and are known by them. The role of the service is to enable people to continue to use their local facilities so that ongoing contact with neighbours can deepen their relationships and sense of community.

- People also form bonds because they share particular interests, even though they may not live in the same locality. They meet around recreational activities, religion, politics, or work, which give them a common sense of purpose. Those we support can become part of such groups too.

STRATEGIES FOR BUILDING AND SUSTAINING COMMUNITIES

But, a sense of community does not just happen. It takes a conscious effort to create experiences that draw and hold people together over time. We have to know how to create common bonds, so that people want to take part and become committed. Community psychology[73, 74] and our own experience highlight the following factors:

Have a plan based on shared aims and values

To feel that they have important things in common, people must share similar values and goals. This is helped greatly when a group is clear about its reasons for coming together and plans for what they do. When they are successful in their aims, people feel good about belonging to the group.

Established groups already have aims and values that attract people to join. Thus somebody joining a Special Olympics club is clear what it is about, what is asked of members and what they are likely to get out of their involvement.

New groups that are not part of a larger organisation will need to work out their aims together. These may be simple or challenging, but it is essential that some significant needs of members will be met if a sense of community is to develop.

Help people build a sense of belonging

A sense of belonging comes from getting to know the other people that are involved and feeling accepted by them. So linking people and creating events where they can build relationships is very important. As people develop a sense of belonging they become more willing to invest time, effort, and resources in order for the group to be successful. This may mean making sacrifices and compromising for the common good. Because of that sense of belonging, people feel that they are in 'the right place' and feel secure.

Jack was an enthusiastic member of the local soccer team's supporters club for years. He was made to feel very much part of the club and was included on all the away trips; there was never any difficulty in getting a lift. One day he collapsed at work following a stroke. During the acute phase of his illness he was regularly visited by members of the club who kept him informed of the team's progress. Subsequently, in spite of being significantly incapacitated, he was given extra support by others to maintain his active membership.

Change attitudes through experience

Sometimes without even realising it, people bring unhelpful mindsets about other people to a group without even realising it. The most powerful way of changing such attitudes is through first-hand experience of people's abilities.

A supported employment consortium was set up that included people from the services and members of the local business community. The businessmen and women were keen to help, but had anxieties about placing people in 'real' jobs. They were not confident of the contribution people could make and were worried about tokenism. At times their attitude was unintentionally patronising and' charitable'. Also, they feared that other workers might resent people coming in, and accuse management of using cheap labour that could result in a cutting back of their own hours.

A start was made when Hadi got a work experience placement in McDonalds. As feared, other workers were hesitant in welcoming him and were wary of working alongside him. However his cheery nature made Hadi popular with customers and he won round the co-workers who grew to look forward to having him on their shifts. Although he still needed reminders to ensure the tasks he was given were done, the co-workers were happy to provide this once his job coach withdrew. The manager says Hadi has improved staff morale and made the place happier for everyone to work in. The business members were impressed by the positive feedback, and the supported employment consortium expanded their efforts with a new confidence.

Put the people we support at the centre and draw on their abilities

To build relationships and a sense of community with the people we support, it is essential that they be at the centre of what is happening, not on the margins.

The village had grown a lot in recent years because of new housing develop-ments, but it was felt that newcomers were not being well integrated with the locals. In an effort to build community, it was decided to revive the annual county show, which used to be a popular event. People from the local service were already appreciated in the old village, and thanks to a family member on the committee, it was agreed to involve them in the running of the show in every way possible. They were recruited as volunteers under the direction of the stewards; they were included in judging panels insofar as individuals had the capacity to understand the rules; they welcomed dignitaries and accompanied them during the show; some even did interviews on local radio and in the press. They were much praised for the way in which they fulfilled their various roles in an event that proved a great success. The fun that was had by all helped to introduce new residents to their neighbours, including those needing support.

Keeping people at the centre in this way allowed their abilities to be recognised and created that delightful sense of spontaneity and humanity that so many of them bring to whatever activities they undertake. The show committee became part of a national network set up to revive county shows, and when they visit other places to sell the idea, they bring some supported people with them as a valued part of the team.

Involve people in decision-making

To develop a sense of belonging, people must be made to feel that they matter to the group. They experience this when they are able to influence what is going on. In turn, they themselves become more open to being influenced by the group. People must have opportunities to share in decision-making regarding current activities and future plans. If the group respects individual differences, each member feels valued.

> People attending a day centre wanted to have easier access to community facilities. They proposed having a 'drop-in club' near the shopping centre. A committee was formed of people from the centre, some community supporters, and a member of staff. A disused shop was found and the committee planned its redecoration and furnishing. They made arrangements for looking after the club premises – opening and closing it; cleaning and catering – and they organised the activity programme. All were involved in making decisions and learned to respect each other's opinions. They held interviews for the support worker that the service employed. Everybody was proud of the new club and the way in which it gave people a good base from which to become more involved in various local activities. The centre has been so successful that two others have been opened in the city.

VALUE COMMUNITY SUPPORTERS

People are to be greatly valued when they freely give their time to help somebody have a fuller part in the local community. The people we support form a relationship with somebody who has chosen to be with them. It's not their work; they are involved because they want to be. But community supporters do not usually just appear! The onus is on an organization to seek out people and respond enthusiastically to their interest.

It must be remembered how daunting it can be for a community supporter to come in to special service settings, especially at first. He or she may never have met a person needing support before. The service supporter needs to act as a bridge between the new community supporter and the person being met, until they grow to know each other.

Unfortunately, some service supporters may see community supporters as a threat. It is up to the organization to create an ethos based on the idea that these people are here to *add* to the service's wider goals. They're not a substitute for staff members but are there to enhance their efforts and extend them in ways the paid staff may not be able to do.

It is also important not to burden community supporters with the problems a service may have. The person is coming in to do something enjoyable and wants to have fun, not hear about an organisation's problems. The most important thing is to create an enjoyable experience that the person would want to repeat. The aim is to have somebody leave saying, 'I really enjoyed that. I can't wait to come back again.'

There must be many signs that make community supporters feel valued, from the way they are treated to the roles that they are given. It is important not to shut down their ideas and enthusiasm by a lot of rules and regulations and red tape.

> I have been a volunteer with people for quite a while now, sometimes organising special outings, events and gatherings. Another volunteer and I decided to make one of the gatherings a little bit special, and we went ahead enthusiastically with some new ideas. The response from the service was very negative; we were told that risk assessments had to be done, permission had to sought from the senior manager who turned out to be on long-term sick leave, and so on. We felt very misunderstood and not valued as volunteers.

Most of all, people need to feel appreciated.

> When someone really says, maybe in some meeting or just during the day, like "Hey, that's great what you're doing" that's for me the thing of feeling valued. It's very simple actually.

Resolve difficulties as they arise

Every group has problems from time to time, maybe because one or more members are not adhering to rules and expectations that govern a group. Or people may strongly disagree as to the right way forward regarding some important issue. Tensions may arise also because of personality clashes.

People must have confidence that when things become difficult, the group will work together to seek good solutions because of their shared commitment to their goals. This will not happen by pretending the problem does not exist: instead matters are likely to get steadily worse. Surmounting crises together, completing common tasks, and being publicly acknowledged, are powerful forces in building community.

> Sometime after Adrian, Bob and Carol moved into the new house, a group of local youths began targeting them with verbal abuse. Bob became very anxious and was increasingly unwilling to leave the house. At the next house meeting, attended by their support worker Michael, it was agreed that Michael and

Adrian would visit the home of one of the youths to speak to him and his parents. Following this visit the abuse ceased.

Experiencing forgiveness from others and being willing to forgive others when conflict or hurt arises is an essential attitude. It is important to know that people are accepted and cared about regardless of their human limitations.

Have fun!

Nothing brings people closer together and increases their pleasure in each other's company than being together for an enjoyable outing or a good party or picnic, or just sharing a special meal, to. Any excuse is a good excuse to celebrate – a birthday, a public holiday, a new pet, a job well done. Or maybe there is no particular reason other than it would be good for people to celebrate, especially if they have been going through a difficult time. The aim always is to have some fun, and to make people feel special and appreciated.

Special Olympics clubs are brilliant in the great fun we have! Initially, as leaders we did not look at the social aspect of the things as being part of our remit, but when parents and athletes were asked what they would like, social activities were the big thing for them and they didn't seem to be getting it elsewhere. So now there are social activities once a month, maybe a disco, the bowling alley, cinema, gym, or whatever, often bringing people together from different clubs. If a particular individual wanted to do something different than other people, then we would say to a volunteer, will you do that?

Communication, consultation and sensitivity

All the elements that build a sense of community among a group come about when there is good communication, consultation, and sensitivity. At meetings for example, attention is paid to each person and all are encouraged to contribute to the discussion. Sometimes, despite encouragement, some people can't say their piece, because of the size of the group and particularly around issues of conflict. One-to-one sharing or small informal meetings may be needed, too. These give an opportunity to deepen mutual trust and emotional connections, which are essential to the resolution of misunderstandings and conflicts that may arise.

When most of these elements are present people feel a sense of commitment and responsibility towards the group. They have a sense of ownership and belonging.

MAINTAINING NETWORKS OF SUPPORT

Different networks meet different elements of people's needs for relationship. Here we take a brief look at the usual networks, highlighting where supporters can make a difference.

Family Networks

Maintaining contact with family members after moving from home is a key wish and social outlet for most people. Supporters' welcome of family members who make contact, or the seeking out of uninvolved relations if a person so wishes, makes a great difference. Relations who feel valued and respected are more likely to maintain contact, and find it easier to engage with service settings that may otherwise be alien and off-putting to them.

But the role of families need not be restricted to the family of origin. Services can also establish host family networks that offer hospitality to people seeking breaks from, or alternatives to, home or service settings[75]. Host families may be voluntary or paid, and the length of time spent in them can vary from overnight to fulltime placements, depending on what is on offer or needed. Family accommodation is an attractive alternative for someone who does not wish to live in a group home with other people.

It is the role of support services to set up the systems that link and support both natural and host families. Given the impressive results, it is not surprising that family home sharing is increasingly practiced in Ireland, Britain and North America. Although these schemes started for children, they are now well developed for adult persons with differing needs too[76].

As well as being very popular with those who come to stay, the host families too express much satisfaction. Their own family benefited greatly from the experience of hosting, regardless of the level of support needed by a guest.

> You have to know these children as personalities. They have brought out qualities in our own children that have amazed us. There was a great sense of togetherness during hosting. There were also the funny and not so funny incidents to relate. We discovered their needs were not very different to the needs of our own children – love, attention, and discipline. They had a gift of settling in without any fuss. We have never regretted the many times we have said' yes' when they could just as easily have said ' no'.

The particular intimacy of relationships within both natural and host families have a quality that cannot be substituted in other settings. Children and adults can grow and thrive through them, and their significance should never be underestimated.

A community of peers

For a time it was thought that community integration meant that people needing support should not spend time with each other, but with people who do not have a disability. That was an over-reaction to the era of institutionalisation when people could mix *only* with peers in segregated settings, and to the fear that they would be stigmatised even more if seen in groups.

Now we respect people's choices about with whom they want to spend their time, and not surprisingly it is often with friends who may also happen to need support[77]. Those who report most satisfaction with their existing level of relationships tend to have a greater proportion of other people needing support in their networks[78]. Generally speaking, intimate relationships occur among people who are matched in terms of age, background and interests. This also holds true for those we support, who are more likely to find intimacy among friends with similar abilities.

Their coming together to create a good social life and to support each other is a normal part of integration. It does not exclude other important social relationships. The only question for supporters is about the amount and type of help that people may wish to have in maintaining their peer relationships.

The first thing is to enable those who share interests and social activities to also share workplaces, residences and neighbourhoods, insofar as they wish to do so. Maximising people's choices as to where they work and live, fosters relationships between peers and helps build social networks.

People should be offered whatever supports they need in organising a social life together. This can mean learning to find their way to meeting venues and using public transport. People who want to do things such as go on holidays together may need greater support. The degree of supporter involvement depends on what people themselves want and need.

The formation of self-advocacy groups and the support of advocates are now well accepted, in principle at least. Where they exist, they are important means of empowering people, as we saw in Chapter 3. Through various self-advocacy activities, including meetings, conferences and workshops, people are also building networks with others, not only where they live but also throughout the country and beyond. People may then go on holidays together or swap houses and visit each other's countries.

Circles of support

Some people have the support of a range of people to enable them to have a good community life. Different people come from different aspects of a person's life, such as a fellow club member, a workmate or boss, a church member, a residential supporter, and so on. The circle may include other supported people who contribute to that person's life.

Somebody needs to take responsibility for bringing the circle together. Ideally this would be a member of the circle, but it may be necessary for a service supporter to take that role early on in that development.

From time-to-time the whole group gathers to review how things are going, to celebrate what is good, and to determine what other supports may be desirable. In meeting in this way, those in the circle also strengthen their bonds with each other and may increasingly contact each other outside of meetings, should the interests of the individual so dictate[79].

Existing social and activity groups

In every locality, there are many existing groups of which people could become members, such as sports organisations, various kinds of social clubs, church groups, walking clubs, environmental groups, and other activity clubs.

It helps greatly to be introduced by somebody who is already a group member. But sometimes a person has an interest in a group or activity but no contacts. A supporter may be needed to initiate the contact, either by accompanying somebody on early visits and to initiate the membership process, or by linking with somebody who is already a member and asking him or her to be the link person. We will examine this option in more detail in the next chapter.

GROWING AND CHANGING

Once established, the ongoing success of a group will require a shift of emphasis from pioneering, growth and development, to sustaining and adjusting activities. A change of focus may be required, driven by the changing needs of the members.

> Mary and her friends established a small walking group that met at alternate weekends. Her sister-in-law, Susan, provided transport. Over the years they had enjoyed many outings but latterly members of the group were finding the walking less enjoyable due to a variety of age-related health issues. So they agreed to refocus their meetings on story reading and board games at Mary's home. This change proved to be very successful.

Loss of a valued member of the group can be painful, but it can also provide new opportunities if members are open to change. The person leaving might have specific skills, experience or training not otherwise present in the group. Then the question arises whether to recruit a new member with the same skills, or change the direction of the activities.

> Linda had been recruited through the church congregation to help establish a music club in the neighbourhood. She sang and played the guitar, the piano and tin whistle. Wednesday evenings had become a popular event with people from the neighbourhood, including residents of the supported housing scheme and the small residential unit. Job relocation meant a move for Linda. With no obvious person available to take her place, the group decided to focus on step dancing as Pauline, another member, was a dancing instructor and keen to offer her services. This change led to some members dropping out of the group, but new members were also recruited.

For a group to be sustained, the successful recruitment and integration of new members is obviously vital. New members may bring new experience and skills, but not too many too soon, especially early on. Continuity and change need to be carefully balanced. Integrating into an established group is difficult without the goodwill and support of all members.

Simon had been taken on to run the small horticultural centre following Bob's retirement. A team of 12, seven of whom needed support, had successfully worked the land for a number of years. Soon after his arrival, in spite of being made aware of the need for continuity, Simon proceeded to institute changes in the produce grown and the working practices, without full consultation and agreement of the rest of the team. Working relationships rapidly broke down and ultimately Simon resigned.

The example of Simon is not uncommon in situations where the key elements of community building are not actively worked with. This fundamental issue was not addressed and dealt with in the discussions following Bob's retirement and when Simon joined the team. In addition, regular review and reflection on the group's aims and processes is essential to pick up early signs of discontent.

Along with loss comes endings, and a group or community may reach a point where further activity is not in the members' best interests or no longer serves a need. Then the task is to give it a "decent burial" by celebrating all it has contributed to the lives of those it has served. It may also be time to set about the creation of new opportunities for those that seek them. New people and new groups can bring freshness and renewal along with the required energies.

LIVING TOGETHER IN WAYS THAT ENHANCE A SENSE OF COMMUNITY

Living with other people can bring a special experience of community. Some prefer to live alone and even thrive on it but it's not for everyone. Living with others can express and deepen people's sense of belonging, even among those who do not always find it easy to be together. There is the conversation, jokes and gossip, a listening ear and, hopefully, a shoulder to lean on.

Jane, Michael and Stephen share a home on Maple Road. They each have their own room. Jane's room is en suite, as she needs a good deal of support and depends on a wheelchair to get around. Michael and Stephen share the bathroom as does the sleepover supporter. Work is organised so that each of them can contribute to the life in the house. Michael loves cooking, so he spends every afternoon at home helping to prepare the evening meal. They all like to invite a friend or family member to eat. Jane has two mornings a week helping with the laundry and ironing. Stephen keeps the house clean and tidy the other three mornings and also does some of the shopping.

All these activities are supported by Mary, whose job description specifies her role as supporting them in their tasks, rather than doing the work herself. Jane, Michael and Stephen have formed their own small community with the support of their families and Mary. They look out for each other and enjoy spending some of their leisure time together. As Jane has cerebral palsy and limited speech, Stephen supports aspects of her mobility, travel, recreation and communication. He has no family contacts, so Jane will invite him to her parents' home occasionally at weekends.

It's not all plain sailing, as Michael can be quite overbearing at times. But it's not often Mary, the sleepover care worker, or a family member has to intervene.

Jane, Michael and Stephen, along with Mary, have formed significant one-to-one relationships outside as well as within the group. Living together has also given each of them an opportunity to make a real contribution to each other's lives, to support each other and through that to grow in confidence and self-esteem.

Community-building at home is done through the normal activities of any household, consciously used to engage and affirm people, and to create enjoyable and meaningful occasions. A possible conflict for paid supporters is that a person's home is their workplace. Are they part of the home community or are they apart from it?

Sharing meals

Meals are important times for community building. What better opportunity is there to engage in an activity on equal terms than sharing a meal? Yet, regrettably, in many services it is still exceptional for paid supporters to eat with those living in the house.

There's an interesting dynamic when the six of us sit down to meals: for a start, who's going to bless the meal and how, and then who was going to serve up-- it could be any of us. Michael with his tension, his pressure of speech and his obsessional interests might dominate the conversation. But Jason, with his wry sense of humour or Tessa, with her mischievously repetitive "I like you" or more often "I like Susan", or even "your killing me", interspersed with comments about a new tape or some transient aches or pains, adds to the colour. What could be more natural?

People with more profound difficulties will need extra assistance, but that does not mean that those providing it can't share the same meal. Doing so in some settings may involve a significant shift of boundaries and job descriptions. Paid supporters might not then always be either on or off duty but sometimes both on and off duty!

Caring together for the home

Caring together for the home gives many opportunities for people to contribute according to their abilities. The support given, the teamwork required and the satisfaction of contributing to the upkeep of one's home, and to the well being of those lived with, are all positive experiences, particularly if publicly acknowledged.

In Rose Cottage, clearing up after the meal is always a joint effort. Everyone expects clean dishes for cooking and eating so it's taken for granted that everyone clears the table. Then Therese or one of the supporters wipes it and sweeps up, or washes the dishes, while Sarah and John dry and tidy them away.

Then supporters don't end up doing all the domestic work themselves but focus on what is going on for those they support during household chores. And those supported can learn new skills and perform valued roles that enhance their self-esteem as part of an inclusive team. Such chores are important because there is no difference between supporters and those being supported. Opportunities need to be developed in different contexts around the home and adjusted to suit the abilities of the people living there. Rory, a supporter in a group home tells this story.

> Beth used to sit around in her wheelchair; getting in everybody's way. In the kitchen she parked herself in front of the washing machine so she could watch the clothes go round. One day, I thought there's something she could do – put the clothes into the machine. She needed a lot of help at first as she has difficulty controlling her arm movements. I could have put the clothes in much faster but I just left her to get on with it. I had to close the door and turn on the machine but now she trying to do that by herself. She's also starting to take the clothes out of the machine but finds it difficult to get the ones at the back. We're trying her with tongs to see if they help. Her mother can't believe how much she's come on.

The temptation is for supporters to do all the household chores so that the job gets done quicker and maybe even better. But that misses the point. Working alongside people in these ways, can powerfully affect in very positive ways the attitudes of supporters and those being supported over a period of time[80].

Privacy

To be able to live successfully with others also requires times of privacy, getting away from the group or from some demanding individuals. People need their own rooms, where possible, or at least have the exclusive use of a sitting-room or some other space at times.

House Rules

Living together encompasses all manner of relationships and involves a complex interplay with many "rules", both explicit and implicit. This is necessary because although one's bedroom is usually private, bathrooms, toilets, kitchen, dining and living spaces are generally shared, and each person's behaviour needs to respect the others involved.

As we know, there can be endless sources of friction when one shares a home with others. These problems are not unique to sharing home with people needing support. Nevertheless, there may be particular issues around the ability of those supported to comply with house rules and others' expectations.

> Sarah, Therese and John live in Rose Cottage with Martin and Elizabeth, the householders, and with Stephanie and Christine, two young volunteers. Sarah needs a fair bit of support, particularly in the area of communication as she has no speech, relying on sign language. An issue of contention in the house

has been her habit of entering others' rooms without knocking, sometimes even when the room was empty. Mostly she would simply be looking to see where the person was, perhaps wanting to be with them. Occasionally she has been looking for cigarettes, drinks or coffee which, if found, she has taken. The attitude of the others has been that Sarah can manage this house rule and is expected to do so. After such an incident, this is always put to her and her agreement requested.

The process of dealing with such issues in itself builds community: people have to listen, negotiate and adapt to each other and in so doing, social rules are learned.

House meetings

House meetings are an important way of deciding together about matters arising in the house or planning for the future. Everyone has a voice in a house meeting, and it becomes an important place where people learn to express themselves and listen to others. This is Frank's view on meetings in his community:

I like the Community meeting because it happens once in a while for everyone who is interested in discussing issues that concern all of us. And I enjoy collecting points for it (the agenda). I never thought before that I could chair a meeting and recently had chaired a Community meeting after collecting points for that. One of the things we discussed at the meeting recently was having a family day. We have also discussed sports and the different possibilities for what people like to do when they do sports.

Sustaining people

At times people can find it hard to get along with others. This may be because of personal difficulties or a clash of personalities. This can show itself as aggressive behaviours. A common response to managing a crisis is to move the person out of his or her home. However, if this can be avoided, supporting a person through a crisis can be a very powerful community building process.

Maureen was placed in residential community at age twelve, due to increasingly challenging behaviour at home. Over time she gradually settled in her new environment though things were never easy. However, in late adolescence, her level of tension, aggression and distress escalated markedly. To manage this, a major redeployment and increase of resources was put in place, with the carers working very closely as a team to support her. Within the security of the situation she gradually settled again and the bonds made persisted for many years.

Everyone needs to be prepared to make a commitment to the person for these strategies to be successful. It can help if there is an option for people to move out temporarily to give everyone a break. But the fundamental premise is that people need to be supported in the place they know as home and it needs to be their choice if a move it to happen. In such situations, a high level of support is required, for the sense of failure, loss, and guilt is often considerable for all the parties involved.

Broader issues influencing success

Living together as a community is influenced by broader issues that can profoundly affect the atmosphere of the home and the nature of the relationships experienced. For example: Can the people really choose who and how many people they live with? Have they a say in which paid supporters come to their home and the way in which they support them? Are those who live in the house encouraged or even expected to do as much as they can themselves and for each other, with whatever level of support is required? These and other questions are fundamental to creating a home community rather than housing a number of individuals.

People living independently

Whether by choice or by necessity, some people live alone. They can gain from the sense of independence this brings. However it is even more important that people living on their own are part of community groups that give them a sense of belonging and ways of spending their free time. They need opportunities to form friendships and networks of relationships, and this may need the help of various supporters, whether paid or voluntary. For example they should be included in invitations to events and activities that are being organised for people living in service settings or in the same neighbourhood as them.

> Janet lived alone in a one bedroom flat in a small social housing project. She managed the practicalities of life, including medication successfully. Janet took the local bus every day to her work 30 miles away. She also took the bus home to her parents every weekend. One of the main tasks of the project supporter for Janet was to help her effectively manage communication with her parents around issues of risk and independence, and with her work around issues of health. The other role was to make introductions and support friendships locally, as Janet was new to the town. Although Janet did have social contact with one of her neighbours, she remained relatively isolated and eventually returned home to her parents. This highlights the risk of someone losing their own local networks and the effort required to establish new ones. Perhaps additional supporters, such as a circle of friends, would have helped; people who might visit her in her home, have a cup of tea or meal, or watch TV with her.

There may be a delicate path to tread between invading a person's privacy and providing much-needed support. As always, getting it right will depend to a large degree on the relationship between the supporter and a person they wish to support, on knowing each other.

INTENTIONAL COMMUNITIES

Intentional communities are a particular form of living together, where people and their supporters share their home, work and leisure – as a community. They want to build a different kind of life based on sharing in common rather than individualism, and they seek out others who feel the same. Examples of these communities include Camphill[81] and L'Arche[82], where people with and without a formal disability choose to live together. The mission statement of one life-sharing organisation aims:

> To create communities in which vulnerable children and adults, many with learning disabilities, can live, learn and work with others in healthy social relationships based on mutual care and respect... and on the acceptance of the spiritual uniqueness of each human being, regardless of disability or religious or social background.

People who need support are at the heart of the community, not out of kindness but because their role is such a central one. These communities have discovered that the people often thought of as the weakest in society, far from being a threat or a burden, can be teachers of the heart and a source of new hope.

> So it is that people come together, not because they live in the same neighbourhood or are related, but because of a mutual sympathy; they come together around ideas, around a vision of man and society, a common interest.... They want to bear witness to those values. They feel that they have some good news to offer the world, news which brings greater happiness, truth and fulfilment. They want to become the yeast in the dough of human society. They want to work for peace and justice among all men and all nations[83].

Intentional Communities differ from the more conventional service models in their underlying ethos and elements of their practice. They usually operate independently of professional involvement in their daily activities. The holistic approach means that the different domains of life-sharing such as work, leisure and worship are incorporated to a greater or lesser extent into the life of the communities[84]. This could be viewed as a form of "reverse integration", whereby supporters share the life of those they support. This is not based on a wish to be isolated from the wider community but on the present poverty of opportunity for true integration on an individual level. However, those communities established in urban areas will often tend to be more integrated into their local community.

There is an explicit acknowledgement of the level of interdependence between those needing support and those providing it. Experience has shown that a spectrum of abilities enhances mutual interdependence between everyone in the community. It is recognised that *all* members have needs, and it is the responsibility of each person to respond to those needs to the extent that is appropriate and he or she is able. This interdependence is empowering in that it gives opportunities for those generally perceived as being solely receivers to give and contribute too.

There is thus an unspoken expectation that all members of such communities don't only live together, but also care for each other and contribute to each other's and the community's well-being in different ways, depending on individual gifts, abilities and inclinations. All members have rights and responsibilities and there is a shift from the dominant view that one group of members have "rights" that have to be safeguarded by others who have "responsibilities", to one of "mutual interest" in the context of the life sharing community.

Community members live with each other's strengths and weaknesses, for no one are perfect. But working with that challenge is also the key to personal growth and maturation. All members need to be encouraged to keep an eye out for each other and particularly for those who are perhaps less able to safeguard themselves from common risks and abuse and are therefore especially vulnerable.

> Clare is a very vulnerable and immature young woman who dreams of relationships, marriage and motherhood, and this creates great tensions for her. She is much more likely to share her plans and escapades with her peers like Linda than with her supporters. In this context Linda is in fact her supporter in that she tries to counsel her to the extent that she can but also shares her concerns about Clare with her supporters who can then intervene as necessary.

Life sharing communities are a particular model where those who need support can play a central role in the process of community building. The relationships that develop can have a special quality in that they are based on real-life situations. Reciprocity and mutuality are at the core: the dignity of each member can be upheld, and their unique contribution valued. By having a voice, making a contribution and being given responsibility, people needing support are empowered and can develop a sense of ownership for the community.

Although life sharing communities are different from most other services, some of their characteristic features will also be seen in other organisations, particularly those that aim to do things *with* the people they support rather than only doing things *for* them. Perhaps the most important lesson from life sharing communities is the move towards real reciprocity in relationships between supporters and those they support.

Sharing one's life with people who need support as in intentional communities would clearly not be the choice of most people today, but at the end of the 20th century in the U.K. and Ireland approximately 2000 people live in such communities, of whom about half have an acknowledged disability[85]. This is a small number relative to the total figure of those needing support. But the communities have a significance that is beyond their numbers. They remind us that sharing life means:

– Being alongside people in all the ordinariness of daily life;

– Integrating socialising, work and leisure in a natural way;

– Valuing everyone's contribution;

– Working co-operatively as a group;

– Finding personal fulfilment supporting, and being supported by others.

It's natural

As with relationships, a detailed analysis of community building may hold the danger of making it all seem difficult, needing the input of 'experts.' This is not true. There are many people with an excellent understanding of what it takes to bring and hold people together, and who do so in a natural manner. But, when consciously seeking to build community with and around the people we support, it certainly helps to understand the different elements involved. And these are truly learned only by being put into practice.

JOINING COMMUNITY NETWORKS

For too long, persons with disabilities have been isolated, their right to development ignored, and their potential contribution to society neglected. The cost of denying equal opportunities to persons with disabilities is high, not only in financial terms, but also in the loss of their contributions to society.... The untapped potential of disabled people will be realised only when governments ensure that equal opportunities are given to all of their citizens.

United Nations Standard Rules on the Equalisation of Opportunities for Persons with Disabilities (May 1994)

This chapter builds further on the theme of supporting people to become part of the networks within their local communities, both as users of community facilities and as members of social groupings. The strategies we described in Chapter 6 apply here too but we need to extend them if we are help people fit into existing groups and settings, especially when the people in them may have little prior experience of people who need additional support. We identify five key means that supporters have found successful and we look at how these strategies can be implemented in two key areas; work and leisure. Finally we look at four formidable barriers that can deter people's social participation.

COMMUNITY VISIBILITY

At the outset we need to note that merely providing support services in community-based settings is insufficient to ensure people's social inclusion within those communities. It is however, a pre-requisite. There are many greater opportunities for social integration when people live in ordinary neighbourhoods rather than in remote hospital or residential centres. Yet that is still a reality for some and their physical exclusion must be ended before we can really address their social inclusion.

People become visible to others in the community when they use the same facilities and services. In the past this may not have happened as specialist services were provided for people with particular disabilities. This not only increased people's invisibility to the wider community but it had an added detrimental effect. Staff working in mainstream health services, for example, did not have the opportunity to extend their knowledge and expertise to people with additional needs, thereby increasing their feelings of inadequacy when faced with these patients. The same argument applies to education and workplaces as well as to social and community groups within our society.

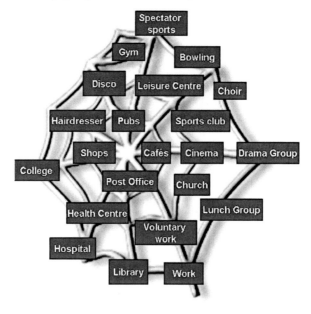

Figure: Community facilities used in Northern Ireland

Thus at its most basic, community networking means using the facilities and services that are available for everyone within communities. The Figure shows those commonly accessed by people with intellectual disabilities in Northern Ireland[86].

In many instances people are accompanied by supporters when they go to these facilities. Their assistance may always be required: to assist with travelling, communication and handling money for example. However there is a danger that supporters can get in the way of people interacting with others and prevent them being seen as a person in their own right – be it as a customer, patient, student or whatever. Instead the image others see is someone who is different, dependent or disabled. This is even more accentuated when groups of people are taken out with one or two supporters. It is therefore a delicate balance that supporters have to maintain when using community facilities: between providing the support that is needed yet leaving the person the freedom to be like others. We will return to this point later.

Community networks can mean something deeper. They are ready–made groups which when people join, gives them the sense of belonging and identity which we described in the previous chapter. This does not happen easily or speedily for the people we support. The reasons have been covered already: communities are wary of 'strangers'. In a sense, supporters are much-needed 'go-betweens' who can assist people to join the networks of their choosing. And as we said earlier, they need to withdraw at the right time and leave the group to get on with it; otherwise the danger is that people are not accepted as members in their own right.

Despite the importance of community participation to the people we support as we noted in Chapter 2, for many supporters and services, it is still seen as an optional extra when they have the time or the inclination to do it. It is not viewed as a priority in their work[87]. Such attitudes need to change. Community networking is an imperative placed on all supporters and one for which we will be held increasingly accountable in the future.

We begin by reminding you why supporters need to tackle this issue, difficult though it can be.

WHY JOIN NETWORKS?

Four clear reasons can be given.

1. As citizens, everyone has the right to participate in the opportunities that society provides. Many countries have laws that make it illegal to discriminate against persons on the grounds of disability. These apply in education, in employment and to all public services.

2. As we saw in Chapter 2, people we support often aspire to a better life and see this coming about through participation in the opportunities that others enjoy. In the past, specialist services tried to re-create similar experiences through training, sheltered work and segregated leisure pursuits but as we know these tended to isolate rather than integrate people into society.

3. The benefits that participation in mainstream society brings to people are increasingly evident in newspaper reports, personal stories and research studies. This is no longer an untried and risky endeavour but one that should be open to all.

4. The prejudice and negative attitudes which even today people still experience because of their disability are challenged when they have personal contact with people who up till then, they know solely as a label. The avoidance of social contact means that prejudices are maintained. A father of a teenage boy with Down Syndrome explained it thus:

> Whenever we go as a family to a restaurant I always pick a table in the centre of the room. I want others to see how well my son can cope. It is not good to hide them away. They need to face up to other people's stares and nasty comments. It's something they may have to live with but it's better it happens when we are around to support them rather than leaving it to when we are gone – how would they cope then?

ACCESSING COMMUNITY FACILITIES

It seems so simple and straightforward for us to make use of community facilities that it can be difficult to appreciate the complexity this presents to the people we support. At one level it is easy for them to 'tag along' leaving us to do all the hard work! This has the value of getting people out of the house and being in the company of others. It also gets them used to different surroundings and experiences. But there is the danger of perpetuating a dependency on supporters for their access to community life.

The challenge is to move beyond the 'tag-along' level so that we support people to do more for themselves. The same guidelines for supporting people that we noted in earlier chapters are just as applicable here when it comes to accessing the range of facilities noted in the Figure above, whether it be supermarket shopping, attending a football match or going to the gym.

Choices: People make the choice of which facilities they use and the times when they can do this.

Planning for the activity: People are prepared so that they know what they will be doing, what they need to bring with them and important things to remember. They can rehearse what they will be doing with their supporter. The use of digital photographs taken on previous visits can be a useful prompt.

Graded help: People should be left to do what they can confidently do for themselves and only given assistance with the parts they find difficult. Supporters can position themselves a little way behind the person so that he or she is the focus of attention in conversations with others.

Review and Practice: Supporters can review with the person what went well and lavish praise as a means of building up their self-confidence. Lessons learnt and specific points for improvement can be identified. Further opportunities for practice are usually needed until the person can manage totally on their own.

By this point the role of the supporter is more that of a companion – holding back and leaving the person to get on with it but nonetheless keeping a watchful eye and being ready to step in if help is requested or required. In due course, and if it is judged safe to do so, the person can go-it-alone or in the company of a friend, although they may still require help with certain parts, for example getting a lift by car to and from their home. Learning to use a mobile phone, of which there are now very simple models, can be a helpful asset too.

These same steps can cover the use of all sorts of community facilities: visits to the health centre as well as outings to the pub and going to the cinema or to the library. Indeed the skills acquired in using one facility will help people become competent users of others.

But supporters can experience two pressures in these settings that may be less evident than in other aspects of support.

First, their support is being provided in the public eye and they may be concerned about what others think of them as supporters, for example not giving the help that others would expect them to give.

Second, they may be concerned that the person would let themselves down in some way: they don't want them to fail or do something 'silly'. It is less risky if the supporter takes the lead.

These pressures can be eased through experience and with the advice of other colleagues but ultimately each person has to find a way of dealing with their own fears and uncertainties.

JOINING COMMUNITY GROUPS

Thus far we have focussed on people simply being present in, and in using community facilities. There is though the further step of getting to know and to be known by other people. Here we have in mind social, leisure and work groups some of which can consist of small numbers of members while others are much bigger.

Joining groups that already exist is an experience we all have had in our personal lives, from childhood onwards. Some people find it easier than others to join in. What's different this time is that you are supporting other people to do this. If left to themselves, they may not have the resources or capacity to make the necessary connections; although there are some who are well able to do so.

There may be a further complicating factor. People within the community may be meeting people with special needs for the first time. Research tells us that they may feel anxious and uncomfortable, unsure of what to say or do[88]. This anxiety can lead to people avoiding personal contact and in extreme forms can result in rudeness and insults. Their apprehensions can be much reduced if meetings take place in a planned and purposeful way, perhaps based around a shared activity in familiar settings. As we noted in Chapter 5 supporters are uniquely placed to act as a 'go-between' between people who are new to one another.

Once you have identified the person's particular interests and aspirations, there a number of steps that will help their joining. These are intended to cover a variety of situations be it joining a choir, yoga class, sports club or a group of workmates

Obtaining information

First, you need to know what's available in your community. If people cannot read or use the Internet they are immediately disadvantaged in knowing the options that are available to them. Supporters need to seek out information and pass it on: whether it is by reading local newspapers, joining mailing lists, looking at notice boards or simply chatting with others. Moreover they should be able to signpost people to other sources of information on what's available in their locality, such as volunteer centres, leisure centres and citizen advice bureaus. You might also be able to ring around your personal contacts whom you think could advise.

Making introductions

Once a community activity or event has been identified the next hurdle is getting there and going into a roomful of strangers! Having the company of another person can help on both counts and if that person already knows people in the community group so much the better. The supporter can introduce people by name and help to assist conversations so that people can get to know more about one another. Particular thought needs to be given to overcoming any communication difficulties that the person may have.

Emphasising competence

New people joining others for the first time need to create a good impression to increase their chances of being welcomed. Physical appearance, manners and social graces all play their part and astute supporters will have advised accordingly. Opportunities can be created in social settings for people to talk about their interests and reasons for coming to the group. For more formal meetings, such as going for job interviews, practice role plays can help to prepare people for the types of questions they may be asked.

In certain contexts, such as work or educational settings, people may need ongoing support to help them participate competently. Specialised supporters such as job coaches or learning support assistants may be available to do this as we describe later.

Identifying community supporters

The supporter made need to accompany the person for a period of time to assist him or her in managing the new situation and participating in it. However the goal is for the supporter to eventually withdraw so that the person and their co-members take on these responsibilities. A useful bridge is to find a member of the group who can act as a community support (sometimes known as a natural support) for the person. This person can assist if a helping hand is required. This strategy has been very effective in helping people within work settings in particular. Often these pairings arise spontaneously and without too much effort. It's surprising just how many people have some previous experience or contact that spurs them to volunteer to take on this role.

Providing advice

Once the joining phase is over, the supporter who instigated the contact has a continuing role to play in being available to give advice and reassurance should anything remiss happen or difficulties arise. Leaving a contact phone number or making occasional phone calls to members of the group are useful ways of maintaining contact but always with the full knowledge of the person you are supporting.

Whose role?

The broad approach we have outlined has proved successful in assisting people to join in various sorts of community networks and it is applicable too if people want to join groups specifically set up for people who have special needs. Nonetheless it can be a new endeavour for many existing supporters whose contribution has mainly been within the person's home and not in accessing and joining community networks.

In some areas, this role may be undertaken by other supporters who have a specific function, such as helping people into employment or to take part in leisure activities[89]. There is merit in people having access to additional supporters especially if they have relevant experience and expertise for the task. But if this type of resource does not exist, the supporters who are available may need to take on a community-networking role. There are training resources to prepare people for such roles[90].

In the remainder of the chapter, further examples are provided as to how people can be networked into particularly significant activities that are available in all localities, starting with arguably the most significant of all, work.

PRODUCTIVE WORK

In our society, work is a primary route for community networking. Notice we use the word 'work' rather than employment. If we take a broad view of work, then the potential for people to find a place in a working environment is very much greater. There are opportunities in homemaking and domestic work, in gardening and land work, in craftwork and arts pursuits. People may undertake voluntary work in their neighbourhood or go on work experience placements. They can be supported to find paid employment in the open job market and some may even start their own businesses. Some detective work by supporters can uncover more opportunities than is commonly thought.

Patricia is a young woman with severe epilepsy and mild cerebral palsy. She is also significantly overweight. This combination of difficulties restricts her mobility and her manual dexterity is also poor. Yet in the kitchen at home, which is her working environment, her contributions are highly valued. With a huge effort and perseverance, she manages to chop the vegetables with support, ready for the meal. For this she is rightly proud. And her sense of humour and social engagement are second to none- she loves the banter and jokes.

Whilst Patricia helps with the cooking, Carl is busy ironing at the other side of the large kitchen; company is important whilst working. Loading and unloading the washing machine, and hanging the laundry out to dry before eventually taking it down and folding its are all tasks he manages, so that with minimal support he can responsibly care for much of his own laundry and others' in the house too.

Experiences such as these can transfer from the home into work that can be undertaken in a voluntary capacity, such as helping with meals-on-wheels, or in part-time paid employment, for instance doing the laundry at a local B&B.

Benefits of work

Money is not the only motivation for work. Being identified as a "worker", such as a cook, a gardener or a cleaner, all give people a sense of self-esteem. Enjoying the work, and seeing its value and meaning are also important aspects. Doing it alongside others in a social context, being appreciated and respected for one's effort and contribution are further benefits.

After increasingly difficult behaviour that constituted a significant danger to himself and at time to others, Steven found himself in a locked psychiatric ward and occasionally in their isolation room. His passion (obsession) had always been tractors and to a lesser extent lawnmowers, and he was used to spending time around farms. Through the support of a "job coach" Steven was slowly able to make the transition from the psychiatric ward to a social therapeutic smallholding. Grass cutting was his job and minding the fire where rubbish was burned was another. But he also slowly found that working alongside his job coach at the ditching and a variety of other jobs around the farm and garden could also be rewarding.

Over time his sense of responsibility for the farm, and the knowledge of what was going on there increased steadily and with it his self-esteem as he saw that he had an important role to play. Steven has come a long way but there are further miles to be travelled as he slowly learns to deal with his frustrations and acknowledge his responsibility to stay with his work even when it doesn't always suit him.

Training for and success in work over time will always have more general benefits in terms of the ability of the person. Ancillary skills that are also gained as one learns one's "trade", such as increased eye-hand coordination, concentration, and team-working.

> Katie had attended a day centre since leaving school 20 years ago. Her day was filled with tabletop activities such as jigsaws and colouring in. Despite repeated attempts by staff she never mastered being able to write her name. She was selected to go on a new work experience scheme in the canteen of the local factory. Her job was to clear tables and wash dishes, which she became so adept at doing thanks to the on-the-job learning she received from her support worker. The manager, in recognition of her contribution, offered to pay her and Katie was thrilled when the pay packets were handed out the next week and there was one for her. But before she could get it, she had to sign her name on the tally sheet as the other staff were required to do. Undeterred Katie took up the pen and made an attempt at a signature. Later that day, she was seen with pen in hand, busily practicing her writing. By next payday and with some help from the other staff, she was able to passably sign her name.

Associated benefits of working the community include getting out and about rather than being stuck in at home or in a day centre. It means meeting other people, interacting and perhaps working alongside them. It's an opportunity to make friends and experience new kinds of relationships. Work too provides opportunities for creativity and growth that are not readily available in other ways.

> Hanna is a young woman with a mild learning disability who has been cruelly afflicted with serious epilepsy for which brain surgery left her with a significant speech impediment. To compound her difficulties she also developed rheumatoid arthritis. Hanna enjoys weaving: she is a very conscientious and careful worker and has become an accomplished weaver. This gives her a great deal of satisfaction, and has boosted her self-confidence immeasurably. Recently she took a major step and moved into her own home where she receives the support she needs to live more or less independently.

Of course being paid the rate for the job is increasingly seen as the right of all workers. A wage gives a tangible affirmation of one's worth. For some of the people we support this also applies, although others will have little or no notion as to the value of money. However paid work does make them better-off with more money to spend on leisure pursuits for example. But it is crucial to match the job to the person's interests, as pay alone may be insufficient incentive to keep them at the job.

> Jason had quite a temper and a short fuse. He had stuck with his part-time job in Tesco's until a new manager was appointed and after an altercation with

her, he resigned! He missed the cash though so he went back to the employment agency to get help with finding another job. He had a particular fascination with motorbikes. He owned a bike and was always keen to be involved with any adjustments and repairs it needed. So the idea of a job at the local bike shop appealed to him. Mike, who ran the shop with a part-time assistant, was willing to give it a go. The job description was hammered out: (bringing the used bikes out for display and taking them back in; cleaning the bikes as they were unpacked and sold; oiling and greasing all the bikes brought in for repair); hours, rate of pay and start date were agreed. Initially Jason had his job coach training him full-time. This requirement was reduced and phased out after one month. By all accounts he is a valued member of staff and his outbursts are much less frequent.

Admittedly not everyone wants to work. Some could be considered 'work-shy'; they simply prefer to draw whatever allowances are available to them and enjoy a life of leisure. Others have no experience of working and may lack the self-confidence required to even try.

The type of work might also be an issue: often the people we support will be offered simple, repetitive work. Some people will manage that well, particularly if a suitable social context is provided. Others might be bored and turn down such work or give it up after a time. Likewise when the demands of work appear too great or the person's attention span is limited, they may opt out from the job. Disputes with co-workers or the 'boss' may also cause people to give up.

Thus supporters may expend as much effort on motivating people to take on work as on supporting them in work. Matching the work to people's interests and aptitudes is an important starting point. Even if they have very unrealistic outcomes in mind, these should not be dismissed too readily. Julie, the manager of a specialised employment service tells the story of John who had to be suspended from the day centre he attended because of his aggressive behaviour. He didn't see himself as disabled.

John was fascinated by aeroplanes and his ideal job was to be a pilot. His support worker (known as a job coach) found that too daunting a challenge but decided to follow up options at the airport. She walked around the terminal, inside and out, noting the different jobs that were available there. One possibility that she thought might appeal to John was tending to the plants. She asked the airport manager if he might go on a work experience placement with the gardening crew. At first, the job coach went everyday to help him to learn on-the-job but she gradually reduced the number of visits and relied on his co-workers to provide any support he required. After six months, he was taken on as a part-time, paid worker and joins the plane spotters when the job is done for the day. He has become acquainted with a few of the pilots and they greet him as they come and go.

Training for Work

People can benefit from taking training courses that will prepare them for work. These are often available through Further Education Colleges or specialised training agencies[91]. Training for work has two dimensions. One is acquiring the skills that are needed for a specific job, such as catering, hairdressing, office skills. People can obtain a vocational qualification on the successful completion of these courses that affirms their competence as potential employees.

A second type of training involves the more generalised skills involved in holding down a job, such as literacy and numeracy, communication and social skills, and work related skills such as time keeping, maintaining productivity and such like.

Work experience placements have an important role to play in both sorts of training. This can start with short visits to a working environment and then build up into day or even weekly placements, such as happened with John.

Supporters going along with people at work can be helpful in developing the first elements of a work ethic: the ability to get to work on time and stick at it, even if it isn't necessarily what they wanted or thought it would be like. Achieving this work ethic is probably one of the most important requirements for breaking into the job market and keeping a job. This process of acclimatisation can be started while still at school or during further education and training in college or elsewhere.

If people have the chance to experience different working environments it gives them a better understanding of what working involves as well as the range of jobs that are available. Decisions about taking further training courses are then more solidly based. This turns on its head the old notions of first training a person and then trying to find them a job. Now we try to find the job and then train the person!

Voluntary work

Voluntary work provides another opportunity for people to spend time making a productive contribution in a realistic working environment. For many people who don't cope with pressure, this is an ideal solution; the days and hours they work can be flexible suiting their needs at any given time. The options are widespread, as a visit to a local Volunteer Bureau will identify. Among the popular options are assisting in charity shops, working with animals and catering for community groups. However people's contribution needs to reviewed and not continued indefinitely.

Allan was keen to try work experience in the local nursing home. There was a possibility for him to help with the teas, but his real task was to help one or two of the residents take a small walk and to talk to any residents looking for company. These latter requirements were real needs that could not be met by the care staff due to lack of time, but could potentially make great difference to the quality of life of the residents.

Allan agreed to work two mornings a week. Being a very sociable and caring young man, Allan loved the work and did well. He was able to sustain this over a period of almost two years. However, there were many days when Allan didn't manage to attend; on some occasions he would have been in hospital or attending appointments, and on other occasions he simply didn't feel up to it. Eventually it became clear that Allan was no longer enjoying his time at the nursing home and with support he was able to submit his resignation and negotiate a reasonable period for working his notice.

Although voluntary work places no particular demands in terms of productivity, there is an expectation that the person is sensitive to the ethos of the working environment and does not disrupt it. This in itself is a valuable experience. It can help the person to learn to differentiate and respond differently to the situations they are in. Invariably there are opportunities for friendships to grow.

Supported employment

The opportunity to be actively involved in choosing and working towards a career is a right for the people we need support. Although this remains a viable option for a small minority at present, many of the people we support could manage to work in the open job market if that were their wish and they were given the opportunity and support needed.

Supported employment is the main model that can facilitate this, with the aim of placing people into paid work in an ordinary setting. The criteria for supported employment are not determined by disability: rather a candidate's abilities in relation to their chosen job options are looked at. Once the job is chosen and the necessary arrangements made, on-site training and ongoing monitoring and support by the job coach are the enabling factors[92]. These are supplemented by explicit strategies to promote social integration.

After leaving her special school, Ashley attended a vocational training centre during which she undertook a placement in a factory canteen. Her main tasks were clearing tables and washing dishes and she got on well with her co-workers. When she heard of a part-time job going at local café she decided to apply with the help of her job coach. They helped her to prepare her CV and undertook practice interviews. The café owner was impressed and when the job coach offered to train Ashley on-the-job over a period of weeks she decided to offer Ashley the job. At first the job coach came each day and trained Ashley in what she had to do. Gradually her visits were reduced as Ashley showed she was a competent worker. She is now paid the same hourly rate as other part-time staff.

The job coach also assists with any adaptations that might be required to the working environment and can negotiate adjustments to the workload if necessary. Another key area is helping the person integrate socially with their co-workers and finding a staff member who might act as a community supporter for the person.

There is now much evidence describing the benefits of supported employment for employers, work colleagues and the public[93]. They have the opportunity to experience first-hand the positive contributions people needing support can make. They get used to being with them and working alongside them. Prejudices and fears can be left behind, and instead there is the chance to enjoy the company and gifts of people who perhaps they previously avoided.

LEISURE AND RECREATION

Although work has a vital contribution to make to people's lives, it is not an option for everyone. Yet doing nothing is not a welcome alternative. Equally workers need times to relax. Active leisure pursuits are aspects of a healthy lifestyle; they give a tonic to body, mind and soul. Exploring the leisure and creative likes and dislikes of the people we support, particularly those with more profound disabilities and communication problems, is thus essential. Moreover sharing leisure and creative activities gives people reasons to communicate with each other, build relationships, and hence community[94].

We want to highlight five areas of leisure that are particularly significant for many of the people we support. These are all the richer when done in community contexts.

Exercise and fitness

In common with the wider population, obesity rates are increasing among the people who receive support. Improved nutrition is an important factor in reducing this trend but so too is increased exercise. Although individuals might plan their own exercise regime, people are more likely to enjoy it and stick with it when it is done in the company of others. There are plenty of opportunities for doing this in most communities from yoga to line dancing; football to swimming.

> David is a good swimmer and also loves going to the local pool. He gave up after some local lads gave him a hard time due to his obesity. Since then, he took the initiative and has joined Weight Watchers. So far he's managed to shed a steady one to two pounds per week with an overall weight loss in excess of two stone. He is full of praise for the woman who runs the group whose enthusiasm and humour has kept him moving down towards his target. A recent trip to the swimming pool passed off uneventfully so he's also back swimming again.

Life-long learning

The people we support have the right to education and not just in their childhood. Appropriate further education and training can do much to alleviate the skills deficit of the people we support in areas such as literacy and numeracy, money management and use of computers. Being part of a learning community brings many other benefits too, not least that of making friends. We learn too the need for discipline and the value of co-operative effort.

Another important area of adult education is to give people a sense of their citizenship and of the rights and responsibilities that go with it. Courses are now being developed to cater for this need by Colleges and Universities and by advocacy groups[95].

> **The National Institute for Intellectual Disability at Trinity College Dublin** offers a two-year, part-time Certificate in Contemporary Living. There are three aspects to it: academic learning, personal growth and career development.
>
> The modules focus on developing skills from money management to literacy, personal effectiveness, ICT skills and spoken communication. The expressive modules allow the students to access their artist side, to explore the world of the arts and personal development.
>
> Also in the Inclusive Studies element, each student is facilitated to attend undergraduate lectures in a study area of interest.
>
> Similar programmes are offered in other universities in Canada and Australia.

Arts and crafts

Some people have a particular talent for art or crafts, such as painting, clay modelling, photography and weaving. These are better nurtured among like-minded people than done as solitary activities at home. In some localities, deliberate attempts are being made to make the arts accessible to persons with special needs[96]. Here's the experiences of Lorna and George.

> I lived in a special centre for 26 years and then I decided to move on. I was working in the garden in the morning time, and, and in the afternoon I was doing pottery; making bowls, jugs, cups you know everything; and then I got fed up, you know, doing the same thing, the same thing, the same thing.

> I went to art college in Kilkenny for six years. I remember once we had to go to the castle to pick up a chestnut and then we had to go and draw it and I thought, I thought that was really hard. But not now, now I've learned everything. I like painting, I like sheep, sheep in the woods, I paint swans sometimes or roses in cups. At the end of the year, now, everybody in the class has to do an exhibition and this year, three teachers came to me and said "I want you to put some pictures on the ground and then we'll pick them to get framed" The exhibition is to sell your work and if you put on the wall it's not yours any more. I sold some pictures, I have sold six and they cost 180 Euros. So now I'm saving money now.

JOINING COMMUNITY NETWORKS

George had been creating art for many years, using cardboard boxes and other found objects before training with a stone sculptor in KCAT. He now works in an Arts Council funded studio at the Art & Study Centre, together with other artists. Three hours per week are set aside for each of the studio artists to work on a one-to-one basis with a mentor artist. They work on their own themes towards solo and group exhibitions in Ireland and abroad and take on individual and group commissions. Recent group commissions are a series of 75 paintings for two new hotels in England and the interior design of the chapel/quiet room of Dundalk Institute of Technology.

Kilkenny Collective for Arts Talent (KCAT) began as an EU funded project to facilitate the artistic and personal development of individuals with a range of disabilities. KCAT also provides a full time and part time VEC art courses. These courses are open to anybody and give students the option to work towards a level 2 Art Certificate. Drawing, painting, printmaking, sculpture and photography are part of this, as well as drama classes.

KCAT organises exhibitions and other events, an annual art summer school, weekend and evening courses and workshops for children. KCAT has produced two video animations and a series of outdoor willow sculptures.

Music making

Music is a unique way of bringing people together, either as appreciative listeners or budding players. Particular talents are not always called for and all can play some instruments like drums. Again there may be a range of options available in your locality. Sometimes the atmosphere and setting is as important as the music.

The folk club is quite informal and meets in Cooney's, the local pub, on Tuesday evenings. John gets a great deal of satisfaction from ordering and paying for his own drink, chatting to Mike at the bar or anyone else within earshot, and then sitting watching and quietly joining in by humming the tunes. Irene is more expressive and invariably volunteers to sing a song when the offer is made. She keeps the tune but doesn't manage to get the words out but doesn't mind in the least when others join in.

Drama and dance

Taking part in drama or dance productions offers people the chance to display their talents and bask in well-deserved applause. The interdependence of cast members in learning parts and rehearsing scenes is a hugely valuable community building exercise that can be fundamentally inclusive with people of all abilities, be it as bystanders or in staring roles.

The award-winning *Blue Teapot Theatre Company* in the west of Ireland aims specifically to build community through the use of various arts and personal development activities. It is made up of two parts. The theatre company of supported actors stages its own productions and is involved in joint drama projects with community arts groups. As a result, some Blue Teapot actors have become members of Macnas, the renowned street theatre company. Blue Teapot also devises touring educational theatre for audiences in services throughout Ireland. There are also drama workshops attended by up to sixty people each week.

> Martin has had a troubled life and is a bit of a loner, but as he began to establish himself with community theatre, he found a new sense of being part of something, and his confidence greatly increased. He needs variety in his life, and was not good at his work that changed little from day to day. So he loved being part of different drama events. Martin's supporter reports that his self-esteem has gone through the roof. "He was telling me last night that acting is his job now, and that he is not looking for any more employment now that he is an actor. He has always been aware that he has a disability, but he does not feel like that when he is doing drama. His acting is what matters, and the priority is how good he is at it." Equally important to Martin were the people he worked with: "Why do I keep coming back? "Cos the people are very nice; It's nice to work with this bunch of people."

Some drama groups have put their talents to other uses. They visit schools to portray the effects of bullying. Or they take part in staff training events and conferences to show people what it like to be treated by some professionals.

BARRIERS TO COMMUNITY NETWORKING

We have emphasised the gains that can result from community networking in general and through work and leisure in particular, but equally we acknowledge the barriers that can prevent it becoming a reality for all of the people who need support. In noting the five that are commonly recounted[97], our aim is not to dissuade you from pursuing this goal but rather to spur you on to thinking of how they might be overcome if they are ones you encounter.

Lack of people

Because of the personal support that many people need, often there aren't enough people to provide it. Certainly this is so in many service settings when staff resources are constrained and are even being reduced to save on costs. Hence our emphasis in Chapter 5 of creating networks of supporters that extend beyond paid staff; drawing on volunteers, family members and community personnel to provide the extra assistance that is required.

Lack of money

Participating in community activities can be costly. The people we support often have little disposable income. Their reliance on social security benefits may cover the essentials of life but leaves little for socialising. Even when they receive wages for working, they may be only marginally better off due to loss of benefits. Nonetheless any boost to their income is welcome and so this may be an extra incentive for people to undertake paid work. Low cost options for community participation can be used and all available discounts sought, along with revised budget planning so as to free up some necessary cash.

Independent travel

Travel is another obstacle to people accessing community facilities or work. Given that public transport, rather than taxis, is the most cost-effective option, then learning to do this independently must be a key learning goal for the people we support. Many can master it if the learning is done in a planned and systematic way. A number of training packages are available[98] and with the help of digital cameras, they can be tailored to the specific transport options available in a person's area.

> Gordon was keen to travel on his own by bus. The staff in the training centre he attended agreed to support him in learning to do this. Shona takes up the story: "The staff followed a step-by-step approach and Gordon made great progress. After eight weeks he was able to leave the centre on his own, get on the right bus and travel home by himself. We all took great pride in a job well done and Gordon boasted that he could travel by himself! A couple of weeks later Gordon didn't get off the bus at his usual stop, as he wanted to go into town to do some shopping. But the problems started when he couldn't find the stop in town for the bus home and he ended up on the wrong bus entirely. That was when we realized that we hadn't thought through all that's entailed in being a fully independent traveller. We are now more aware of what precisely the person can do and what it is they still need to learn to do.

Even when people have learnt to travel independently, the lack of transport to certain areas or at certain times curtails their opportunities to attend events.

Dearth of community activities

In modern urban society there are fewer opportunities for people to come together socially. This is particularly so in more deprived housing estates, which is where the people we support tend to live. Likewise in rural areas there is less scope for people to meet unless they are prepared and able to travel the distances involved.

There is no easy solution to this quandary. One approach is for supporters to build a community group around the person as we described in Chapter 6 that may start in people's homes but can reach out into using community facilities.

Another is for specialist centres or schools to open their doors to community groups as a meeting place. The people who attend the centres can then have opportunities literally on their doorstep to mix with others.

Social exclusion

The previous three barriers all have their roots in the way modern society marginalises people who for various reasons are less able. This brings us back to the powerlessness of the people we support and the need for political action to bring about the necessary social changes. In broad terms people's rights are acknowledged but these need to be translated into actions if barriers to social participation are to be removed. Sympathetic politicians and parties in local and central government are needed in order for social justice to be attained.

Throughout human history, societal change has often come about through the actions of individuals. When like-minded persons are prepared to work together they bring about necessary changes that ultimately may benefit all of society.

Change comes from small initiatives which when imitated become the fashion.
We cannot wait for great visions from great people for they are in short supply.
It is up to us to light our own small fires in the darkness.

Charles Handy

WORKING IN PARTNERSHIPS

There is no "I" in team. **Vernon Law**

Supporters need to work in partnership with one another, as this is a better means of supporting people. But such partnerships have to go deeper than social encounters. Two critical elements must be present: team-working and leadership. All supporters need to have a shared understanding of the people they support and common expectations about how their support is offered and delivered. They must build up a shared sense of purpose as this is the basis for effective team-work. Leadership is needed that guides and supports supporters and which co-ordinates their diverse contributions towards common goals.

In this chapter, the focus is mainly on the role of paid supporters who are in the position to instigate and sustain partnerships among all the supporters involved with the person, such as their family, their friends and community helpers as well as other paid supporters.

We acknowledge there has been a strong tradition of disability services working separately from one another and often apart from services that are available to everyone else in the community. This reflects old notions of segregation that have denied many people the opportunities they wanted and needed. A new vision of services is required to meet the challenges of the modern era. For us, partnerships are essential in creating truly supportive services.

ADVANTAGES OF PARTNERSHIPS

We see four broad advantages to partnership working.

Partnerships benefit the person in need of support. They are then less likely to receive conflicting advice or to experience inconsistent reactions from different supporters. They are also more likely to have continuity of support from other people when one supporter is no longer available as often happens when staff leave services.

Partnerships benefit the supporters. A common complaint from staff working in community based services is a sense of isolation and a lack of communication. Similar feelings are reported by family carers. Being part of partnerships makes people less isolated and provides them with others they can turn to for advice and practical assistance. Friendships can be forged and they can feel part of a bigger endeavour.

Partnerships benefit services and systems. Partnerships allow for co-operation and co-ordination, thereby avoiding duplication across services. They enable particular services to focus on what they can do well rather than having services trying to do the work that other systems could do better. Partnerships also contribute to a 'seamless' service for people in need of support.

Partnerships benefit society. Partnership working across communities and systems contributes to what has been termed 'social bonding'. This concept has interested social thinkers and politicians concerned with creating what has been termed 'social capital'[99] in modern democracies where society is increasingly fragmented. They argue that bonding people into discrete communities is but a first step – albeit a vital one which we explored in Chapter 6. But even greater social capital is generated when bridges are formed among these discrete communities and systems. They then become mutually supportive of one another's efforts and together they can have more of an impact when working in partnerships than they do in isolation. Hence they are not only more efficient economically but they build societies in which people can feel they have both a stake and also an influence.

This bridge-building is especially crucial for people on the margins of society, such as those with disabilities. Hence services which aim to support such individuals must be to the fore in creating social capital in their neighbourhoods, regions and countries.

A MAP OF SUPPORT SERVICES

As always, it is so much easier to expound the rationale for partnership working rather than to make it happen in practice. A starting point perhaps is not to try and change the 'big picture' but rather to focus on what is most manageable for us, namely one person at a time! With that in mind, the 'service map' might look something like this.

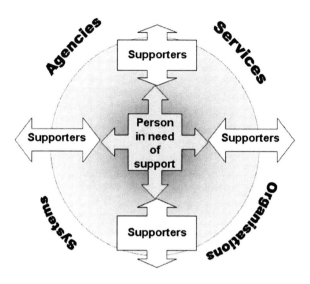

Person-centred

First, the individual in need of support is at the heart of the map. This is different from existing service models in which the core is often a building in which a set of staff work with a group of people who require support, be it a group home, a day centre or a club. And even when there may be no building as such, the central idea is still the provision of services to groups of people who have a common set of support needs. By contrast, we emphasise the personal relationships the person has with their supporters. These provide the basis for the partnership.

Supporters

The second feature of the map are the supporters that surround the person. As we have already noted, one person can have many different supporters as Julie's diary illustrates (see Box). The total numbers will vary from person-to-person as will the mix of different types of supporters. When they work in partnership, they form a circle of support for the person. Later we will examine how these circles of support can be built around an individual. It is worth noting here that for the people being supported, their relationship with the supporters is often the extent of their knowledge about the services who employ them. Management structures, quality standards, policies and procedures may pre-occupy managers and staff but these rarely impinge on people's daily lives.

Organisations

Supporters are drawn from different 'organisations', 'services', agencies, or 'systems' such as social services, educational systems, sports clubs or families. The system to which the supporter is linked will influence their contribution as supporters, which in turn affects the person in need of support. This is especially so with paid supporters as the service system which employs them will have a major influence over the way they do their work. But it can still happen within other systems too, such as the family. A mother's or father's reactions can determine the support that siblings provide.

Julie's diary

On Monday I go to College; do computers, cooking. Tuesday I work in Boots – clearing tables in the café: that's hard work. Wednesday I have a lie in and go to the Club in the afternoon. Oh yeh I make my own lunch. That night its Gateway – see my boy-friend Alan. Thursday it's the centre- that's a swimming day but I've a cold and can't go. Friday it's the centre again; usually I help with the lunches we do for old people. Maria's (*manager of day centre*) trying to get me a cleaning job in the old people's home, then I'd get more money. Saturday's shopping with my support staff and Sunday's church. I help with the crèche. Afternoons I visit my dad and make tea for him and me. He says I'm doing too much but I'm happy. I've people to help me when I need help.

Partnerships need to be forged across these different systems in order to provide a further network of support, this time for the supporters as well as the people in need of support. This outer network of support can prove difficult to achieve, partly because our existing service systems have become large and impersonal. A culture of co-operation rather than competition needs to permeate all these systems.

CREATING CIRCLES OF SUPPORT FOR PEOPLE

However the map shown in the Figure above is only a framework. It must be personalised for each person in need of support as in the example opposite. We start by naming the person, then we can identify the various supporters in his or her life at present, adding in as many support arrows as are needed within the inner circle of support. The result is a map of the support network that is available to each person.

Each map is unique to each person supported – it is their own supporter's club! However it is only a snapshot in time and will need updated as supporters and their associated systems come in to and out of the person's life.

Of course some people will have supporters in common and when this happens there is an even greater need to ensure partnerships are in place. Indeed this can be an important reason for staff in different services to work more in conjunction with others. In time these partnering arrangements may need to be formalised at a systems level but they can begin through the initiative of front-line staff wanting to do a better job of supporting the individuals with whom they work.

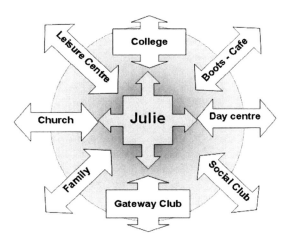

THE DYNAMICS OF PARTNERSHIPS

The dynamics underpinning partnerships are crucial. The arrows on the support map are an attempt to portray these. First, the person provides the heartbeat for the body of support. No longer is it a case of them fitting into whatever support services are on offer but rather the supports they require are tailored to suit them. Hence the person should experience a sense of empowerment: of being listened to, of trusting their supporters and of being at ease and comforted. When these are absent, then it is likely that the dynamics of their relationships with supporters needs attention.

Equally supporters are influenced by the systems with which they are linked. The culture of many service organisations has an emphasis on control and manage-ment rather than autonomy and creativity, on instruction rather than consultation and on decisions being passed down from the 'top' with little regard to listening from 'below'. Consequently support staff can feel dis-empowered, not listened to, distrustful of managers and uneasy in their work. If supporters feel like this, the danger is that they are more inclined to treat the people they support in a similar manner. Nor is a controlling culture conducive to partnership working with other supporters and systems. New service cultures are required if new styles of services are to thrive.

CHANGING SERVICE CULTURES

The term culture refers to the 'unspoken rules' within a service as to how people relate to one another, what is expected of them and how the business of the organi-sation gets done[100]. The concept is equally applicable to voluntary organisations and families.

Culture is something people in the organisation tend to 'feel' and it can be hard to describe but nonetheless it exerts a powerful influence on how staff go about their work. When the culture is challenged, the answer often given for resisting change is: "it's how we do things here". The culture of a service may have evolved over many years and generally it is set by the 'bosses', the people in charge. However the larger an organisation becomes, the more remote the people at the top are from the 'day-to-day' realities. Service cultures persist that are no longer suited to the work that needs doing.

> Tuesday night was Pub night and had been for many years. The tradition was that the five people resident in No. 6 Beechwood Road went for a drink in the lounge bar of the Crown hotel, along with the three staff on duty that night. It was the nearest place to go to, was quiet, and had plenty of space at that time of the evening.
>
> However, both John and Mary had for some time been saying they wanted to go to Murphy's Bar; there was music there and more young folk. The staff response had been that the people had always gone to the Crown hotel, it was the most convenient place to go to, no one was likely to get disturbed or upset there, so everyone could go together to the same place which was the policy of the house.
>
> When Andy joined the staff he took up John and Mary's position, but was only able to affect change when a new manager was appointed to the service. From then on, every week each person was asked where they would like to go and this was facilitated within the limits of available staff and the support needed.

Changing the culture of existing services is not easy but it can be done. The central challenge is ensuring the culture of an organisation is built around the people being supported rather than making them fit into systems that are more suited to others' priorities whether they be management or workers. They need a culture that enables people to express themselves, to grow and to develop. This will give rise to a sense of shared purpose and togetherness across all the people working for the organisation.

In summary then, there are two dynamics at work within the support services we have mapped. One flows outward from the person at the centre and influences the supporters and the systems. The second flows inwards from the services and systems through supporters to the person. Both dynamics are needed for optimal support.

However our primary focus throughout this chapter is on front-line supporters and what can be done to support them in forging partnerships and influencing service systems.

MAKING A START

The most common arguments advanced against partnership working are first: the time and effort required to make it happen and second the differing aims and priorities across the various supporters and systems that makes dialogue and joint working difficult.

These obstacles derive from long-established beliefs and working practices that are hard to shift. This can be just as true for different staff teams within the same service as well as those across different services or agencies. However the first challenge is simply this – how can we bring different supporters into relationships with one another? Here's one approach.

Liam wanted to have a party to celebrate his 18th birthday. His mother initially thought this would be just for his family and a few friends from school but Ian had other ideas! He made up his own invitations and gave them to his teacher, the class assistant, his speech and language therapist, the staff at the short break home where stayed, the leader of the church club he attends and the people he worked with in the café. When his mum started to get phone calls she twigged to what had happened. Her first reaction was to apologise for Liam's actions and then she thought: "what the heck – if Liam wants them to come so be it! Only a few of the people Liam invited came to the party. Those who did had the warmest of welcomes from Liam and he made sure they were introduced to one another.

Social gatherings such as parties, barbeques or dances are a good way of bringing different supporters together. However these don't often happen in modern services maybe because we don't appreciate the need to forge relationships among supporters or to give them a sense of belonging. Instead we try to get by with reference to policies and guidelines or with more formal encounters – staff meetings, case reviews, training courses and so on. These can build relationships if the focus is kept firmly on the persons in need of support, but even then there can be limited scope for different supporters to get to know one another as people rather than in terms of their professional labels and roles.

Partnerships that are intended to support people have to go deeper than social encounters. Two critical elements must be present: team-working and leadership. We will look at each in turn and end by reflecting on new job roles that are needed to facilitate partnerships.

TEAM WORKING

All supporters need to have a shared understanding of the people they support and common expectations about how their support is offered and delivered. They must build up a common identity as this is the basis for effective team-work. This is not an easy task – as any football manager or band-leader will tell you. Individual players have their own ways of doing things and the belief that their way is best! The result is often acrimony and discord, lost opportunities and missed goals, or worse still, own goals! Yet the conditions for nurturing team working are well understood[101]. Fundamentally supporters have to respect and trust one another. Much of the content in Chapters 4 and 5 applies equally to bringing supporters into relationships with each other and creating a sense of community among them. However there are some specific activities that help supporters come together as a team. In brief, these are:

Feeling at ease

People who have met previously or who are given time to chat socially, will find it easier to relax in each other's company and to discuss things with one another. Hence our example at the outset on the value of socialising. People need to come together when things are going well and not just when problems arise. These positive experiences can help people through harder times when differences of opinion emerge.

The setting where you choose to meet can also help to put people at ease. Meetings in homely surroundings can be better than those held in offices.

People can be inhibited in sharing their views and experiences if they perceive others as being more senior or knowledgeable to themselves. The use of first names by everyone is helpful as is skilful chairing of meetings so that everyone is given an opportunity to contribute. With larger numbers, subdividing into smaller groups for part of the time can encourage greater participation and build people's confidence.

Sharing views and expectations

The expectations we have for the people we support and for each other need to be communicated. They might guess at what we believe by watching what we do, but unless we are prepared to speak up and tell others what we think, they will not know for sure. Or worse still, they may think we don't have a view! Thus partnerships start with people who are prepared to share their thinking with others.

Some supporters are reluctant to do this. Many reasons can be given but the main one is often a lack of practice at doing it. Others may be shy and have difficulty in finding the right words. The same strategies can help them to speak up as those we described earlier for people in need of support.

Listening to others

It is just as important to get people listening as it is to getting people to speak up. You can never appreciate what another person is thinking unless you give them a chance to tell you! We need to listen to what other supporters have to say.

More than that, we need to understand what they *mean*. We may need to ask them to explain what's been said or ask questions to help clarify that we have understood. Equally we need the chance to explain our viewpoint and to be listened to in the same way. There has to be a dialogue.

We need to create opportunities when supporters can listen to one another and to the people they support. This can happen informally over a cup of tea, when out on a walk or on a car journey.

More formally it can be done in a meeting, such as team meetings, supervision meetings between a member of staff and their manager, or review meetings when different supporters are present.

Whatever the situation, we need to set aside time when we will not be interrupted. The conversations need not last long if everyone is giving it their full attention.

Discover agreements

In our dialogues we need to start by identifying what we agree on. Too often we skip over this and focus instead on our disagreements. This emphasis can be a key role for 'leaders' of teams of supporters as we will discuss later.

As the discussions continue, people should recap the areas of agreement so that they stick in everyone's mind. It can be a good idea in more formal meetings to write them down on large sheets of paper that all can read. We might also reflect on why it is we agree on the things we do agree on. The answers people give to the innocent question – *"why?"* – helps to identify the things that people consider to be really important.

Name the disagreements

Issues that separate people can be addressed more easily if everyone is clear what precisely the disagreement is. Many a dispute is centred on misunderstandings! The better people are at listening to one another, the easier it is to name the disagreement. When emotions get heightened, people are more inclined to talk rather than to listen. Having a leader or chairperson is an advantage. Their role is to clarify the different viewpoints and make sure that everyone understands the nature of the disagreement.

> **Ground rules for working in teams**
> • Listen as an ally rather than an adversary.
> • Let people complete their thoughts without interruption.
> • Assume the best of one another
> • There are no dumb questions – ask!
> • Raise questions, concerns, issues directly. Don't have the real conversation out in the hall or after the meeting.
> • Try it out! Think about how new ideas might work or as ask questions about making them work before presenting your views about how they couldn't work.
> **Interaction Institute for Social Change (2000)**

Find common ground

Not all disagreements can be solved – people often have to agree to disagree, at least for the time being. Meantime they can get on with what they agree on! Sometimes though, it is possible to find common ground between the opposing views. Each 'side' may have to give a little to make this possible. It's like finding a third viewpoint that everyone can agree on.

Once again, it is easier for people to do this if there is a leader who can guide the discussion towards agreements. But we should all take responsibility for doing this in our dialogues with others. When people start to use phrases like "*I can see where you are coming from*" or "*that's what I've been trying to say all along*" you can feel they are moving on to common ground.

In more formal meetings it is good to write down the common points that have been agreed. Issues that are unresolved should be noted for later discussion.

> The staff team working in a nursing home for people with severe disabilities did not often have a chance to meet because of the shift system. There was increasing friction between the two groups of staff who worked opposite shifts. In order to clear the air, the manager re-arranged the rotas so that there was a one-hour overlap in shifts that could be used for a meeting of all the staff. Before the meeting the manager invited the staff to list all the issues that they wanted to raise. She then grouped the items into those that could be dealt with speedily and those that might take longer to resolve. The meeting started with the easier items and she invited staff to suggest the actions that could be taken. These were recorded on a large sheet of paper so that everyone could read what had been agreed. As the list of agreed actions grew, people became more confident at expressing their ideas. If the group found it difficult to agree on what to do, that item was listed for further discussion at a future meeting. Between meetings staff were encouraged to reflect on the issue and often by the next meeting a solution had been found.

Time away together

Taking a break together, even for a day, is another opportunity for supporters to get to know one another better as they accompany the people they are supporting. Being in new settings, freed from familiar routines, gives everyone an opportunity to explore new ways of relating to one another. A camaraderie can also form that would be hard to create in the busy-ness of everyday life. The time and effort required in planning these breaks can be amply rewarded.

> The community nurses working with families who had a teenager with severe challenging behaviours organised a family break weekend at a residential centre by the seaside, about an hour's drive from their homes. Various helpers were recruited from schools and centres so that a programme of supervised activities could be organised for the young people while parents had a chance to talk to one another and to the various professionals who came along either as visiting speakers or weekend guests. These breaks were a great morale boost for parents as well as giving them the chance to get to know the paid supporters in a more personal and friendly way.

Shared training

If all the supporters involved with the same people can attend the same training events on pertinent issues, this will help to ensure they are working in similar ways and their questions and concerns can be addressed. Opportunities for reflection and discussion should be key features of these training events if they are lead to improved practice and not just the imparting of knowledge.

Celebrating achievements

Coming together to celebrate achievements can be so effective in affirming and cementing team-working. This may take the form of a workshop, seminar or conference that is organised to inform others about the work done and the outcomes achieved. Or an award ceremony and a party may be held. Media publicity in local newspaper or radio might also be arranged as this helps to create a new image for the public of available services.

All the points outlined above apply to all the different partnerships in which supporters can be involved, both within the same team and across different teams. They form the basis for building mutual respect and trust in one another. We may not always be aware of using these strategies when teams are going smoothly but they can be a help in resolving possible sources of dispute.

LEADERSHIP

The second crucial feature of effective partnerships is the leadership that co-ordinates diverse contributions towards common goals, and crucially, also acts as a support to supporters[102]. Any member of a team might be called on to take a leadership role for a particular project or activity even though they are not the formal leader of the team. That's why we have deliberately not used the word 'manager' as we see leadership as a wider ranging function that too often is lacking in services.

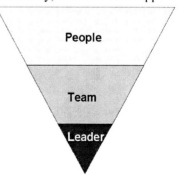

However certain forms of leadership are better suited to achieving particular outcomes. Here we focus on leadership that will ensure people are well supported. Some have called it a 'servant' leadership in that the leader sees him or herself at being at the service of colleagues in building the team and working to achieve its aims. This is the inverse of the usual management diagram with the boss at the top. Instead the leader is supporting the people in the team who in turn are supporting the people. Such leaders have six key roles to play.

Promoting the vision

A leader has a clear idea of what the team is striving to achieve, the outcomes or the results the supporters are seeking to create. They communicate their vision in ways that both inform and energise the members of their team so that they work towards a common purpose. However they do not prescribe *how* they do this. They trust the talents and the ingenuity of their team. They nurture individual's leadership qualities. They are eager to praise people for their achievements in attaining the vision but also to remind them of the priorities if they wander away from them.

'Vision-building' – as it has been called – needs to happen in different ways. Most importantly, team leaders must assist supporters to name the key aspects of their role with the people they are supporting. Hence they will be involved in drawing up their person-centred plans, indeed they may be the leader or facilitator of the process which creates or reviews the plans. In order to do this, they need to know the people who need support and be available to talk and listen to them. But the plan is not the leader's plan. They must not impose it on others. Rather their skill as leader is to have it accepted by all the team members – and other relevant supporters – as their *common* plan.

Leaders must also promote the vision within their team of supporters as they help them to identify the priorities in their work and manage the tensions they may encounter. Again this means being approachable and available to supporters, setting aside time for them to discuss issues of concern.

If leaders are to fulfil these responsibilities to supporters and people in need of support, it follows that the numbers of people in their team must not become too large as otherwise their job becomes very difficult. There is no absolute or ideal number but our experience suggests that a team leader probably can work effectively with up to 25 to 30 persons (supporters and supported persons). In more challenging settings, the numbers will be less.

Vision-building needs to be constantly ongoing and developing, reshaped as people's needs change. Hence the leader should avoid being dogmatic and rigid but rather remain open to an evolving vision that is based around everyone's experiences and contributions.

> The social club for people with special needs was in the doldrums when Simon reluctantly agreed to take over as leader. Volunteers had left and the numbers attending the weekly meetings in the day centre were dropping. Simon called a special meeting of everyone linked to the club. He encouraged people to talk about all the things they didn't like about the club. They went to the local pub to drown their sorrows! There, Simon got them talking about what might happen if the Club was more like a night out at a pub – people mentioned playing darts, games of pool, having a disco, even entertainment! One of the volunteers thought they might be able to meet in the Club she belonged to on Monday nights as few people attended. Later that month the Club was re-launched with a new vision of its purpose and it gained a new lease of life in its new surroundings.

Enlisting the support of others

Vision building needs to occur beyond the persons in the team. Leaders also need to promote their vision with colleagues in other services as well as with family carers but they also need to become connected into community networks[103]. They need to know, and be known by, the influential people within their localities who can open doors to community links. This can mean giving talks to local business groups, becoming members of societies and joining planning forums. Building up such networks takes time and they may not provide immediate benefits but in the longer term they ensure that the community profile of the service is strengthened. These community contacts can become a source for recruiting volunteer helpers, future employees and finding people to serve on the Board of Management of the Organisation, to name but three examples.

These sorts of links are not the sole preserve of leaders, they can also be shared with other service employees. Indeed some of them may already be active in various roles within the local community and leaders may be able to use these to build even more community connections. To some these advocacy tasks may seem daunting but remember we're not expecting leaders to talk about theories or philosophies. Rather their focus is on the people they support and how they do it, topics they know very well and probably no one knows better!

Empowering and motivating

Leaders have to ensure the vision is not just talked about but that it is put into practice. Central to this is the sense of enthusiasm and even conviction they bring to the vision-building, namely, they have a 'can-do' mentality, preferring to emphasise the possibilities while not minimising the problems. They are also inclined to see the glass as being half-full rather than half-empty. They focus on the positives – even when things may seem bleak – as a means of counter-balancing the difficulties that have to be faced. But above all else, they empower people in their team to take on responsibilities, encouraging them to make decisions and to be creative in their work. They will give them credit for their successes and be there to support rather than blame them, if things don't work out as planned.

Working alongside supporters

It may seem like asking a lot of leaders to work alongside supporters but it is achievable sometimes in ways that we can easily overlook. The most basic is simply being with and working alongside other supporters in the team. But the time spent doing this needs to be used for more than socialising – although there should be time for that as well! Working alongside other supporters provides opportunities for leaders to give examples of how they offer support to the person. They can also go on to explain to their colleagues the reasons for their actions. They also have opportunities to mull over other options with them and observe how they offer support. This should provide opportunities to praise and congratulate colleagues for their good practice.

Equally there may be elements of their practice that requires changing but this should be done sensitively and ideally in such a way, that the supporter identifies the need to change for themselves. Judicious questioning can help guide the discussion; for example, what were you trying to achieve, did it work/not work, anything you could do differently?

Time constraints may mean that leaders have to prioritise which supporters they work alongside. New supporters or those who appear to be struggling should have priority. However it is good practice to spend at least one session a year with every supporter on the team. This could be considered a 'mentoring' approach to staff development which although common in other professions is not widely applied in care services[104]. Managers often leave staff to get on with the job – sometimes after little preparation – and rely only on verbal reports about how things are going. People who are masters of their craft have a duty to pass on their expertise to others in practical and tangible ways that others can copy.

> Mairead joined the supported living service as a team leader about a year ago. Her staff team were in crisis although she only discovered this during the first week in the job. Vacancies had not been filled, sickness levels were high, staff were looking for other jobs. Not surprising Mairead found that she had to cover shifts when she couldn't get any replacement staff. However that turned out to be a blessing. As she worked alongside her colleagues, she got to know more about the strains they were under but equally she was able to show them other ways of working and engaging with the people they supported. She deliberately set out to praise her staff and as she did it, she could see them taking an increased pride in their work and even a trace of enthusiasm started to appear – although that was scarce on a Monday morning! Within three months, the team's morale was much improved but Mairead still rotas herself for shifts, especially with the staff she finds it difficult to get on with or to get through to. In giving a reason, she quotes an old saying of her dad's: "Smooth seas never made a skilful mariner".

Reviewing Progress

A fifth key task for effective leaders is keeping check on progress and taking corrective action if things are not working as they should be. In the busy-ness of life it is so easy to keep doing what you have always done, routine takes over and it becomes an end in itself rather than a means to an end. Perceptive leaders are constantly checking out how things are going and making adaptations – often small but necessary ones – as they go along. This can happen over a five-minute chat, by telephone or texting if it proves hard to meet up. Dropping in on people and observing what is happening is also another good way of 'testing the vibes' and catching up on the latest news and developments both from supporters and the people supported.

One-to-one supervision sessions provide other opportunities to review the work of individual supporters and check on any changes or assistance that is required[105]. Likewise regular meetings can be held with all members of the team. These more formal meetings can identify issues that require to be addressed and plans can be drawn up to deal with them.

But most important of all, leaders need to keep track on how life is working out for the people receiving support. Are their person-centred plans being achieved? If not, what's the problem and can we do anything about it? These reviews can be done informally by chatting to the people being supported and their main supporters – either separately or together. Nor should the leaders always take the initiative. Their contact details should be available to everyone so they can be contacted if any of their team members want to talk to them. However more formal review systems may also need to be put in place. For example, a six-monthly review can be undertaken of each person's plan and modifications made in response to recent experiences.

Sharing Knowledge

This last role for leaders emerges from the previous five. They accumulate knowledge, distil the important lessons from it and ensure the insights are shared with all the others on their team.

They strive to know well the people in need of support, their likes and dislikes, what makes them tick, how best to communicate with them and how any problem behaviours are best managed. They encourage others to add to this store of knowledge so that a detailed picture is built up of the person and more importantly, one that is accessible to other supporters. This information may be documented in files but more often it is passed on through conversations and stories.

Likewise, the leader encourages supporters to reflect on their experiences in supporting people, in building relationships or community connections so that they can identify effective actions that can be repeated or ones that maybe are best forgotten. This learning too needs to be recounted to others so that the team's support is more effective in the future. These 'good news' stories are often especially necessary when morale is low. It is also an antidote to uncertainty and hesitation that may discourage others from trying new things.

Knowledge can come from other sources. Leaders may invite staff in other services to visit and share their experiences in meetings. They encourage the supporters on their team to visit other services – especially those with a good reputation – so that they can be exposed to new ideas and other ways of working. They will encourage supporters to attend conferences, workshops or training courses and have them report back to others in the team. They will read magazines, research reports and books as another means of keeping up-to-date and pass on key messages from them to others in their team. They may organise formal or impromptu training sessions around a controversial issue.

When a new training course on personal relationships and sexuality was being devised in a supported living service, a different approach was adopted.

Instead of sending staff to external courses, three of the team leaders in the service were invited to become trainers. In preparation for this, they attended various training courses and visited services in other parts of the country to see how they handled issues around sexuality. They purchased training packs and read various articles. They came together as a team to plan the workshop and to deliver it to groups of staff. Throughout they were able to draw on their experiences in their own service so that the learning was made more applicable. They were also able to follow up in team meetings, the learning from the course and ensure it was applied. This style of training is now practiced more widely throughout the service. Although nervous and reluctant to be trainers, the leaders found this new dimension of their work very satisfying and affirming.

Seeking knowledge takes time and effort from leaders. But given how little we know about providing support, it must be a priority for many years to come.

LEADERSHIP IN DIFFICULT TIMES

An investment in leadership really pays off when problems or difficulties are encountered, as invariably they will. In these circumstances supporters can jump to hasty actions based on mistaken assumptions which may not accord with the vision of supportive services. A thoughtful analysis of the situation is necessary, based around listening to different people's perspectives. When disputes occur, the facts around the issue need to be established and conflicting accounts reconciled. Leaders will strive to take a balanced and fair approach, guiding the protagonists to find their own resolution rather than imposing a solution on them that neither find satisfactory.

But should negotiation and compromise fail, then leaders have to be decisive and prescribe the course of action that is to be followed, ensuring that all parties fully understand the reasons for it. Of course these actions have to accord with the values and aspirations of the vision statement as must the manner of their implementation. Hence the need for leaders to hone these skills in their routine work.

Sad to say, some staff in positions of leadership fail to address service failures or problems. At its worst, problems and conflicts get ignored, bad practices are condoned, and people in need of support are mistreated and maybe even abused. Worse still, with hierarchies of management, these failings can be replicated right to the very top of organisations. Visionary leadership must be present throughout service structures – or brought in if poor practices are to be removed. Equally people in need of support must have a voice at the highest levels and front-line supporters and leaders should be able to speak out without fear of victimisation.

In modern services, visionary leadership is not mainly limited by the talents of staff but rather by the demands which service systems place on them in terms of the amount of paperwork associated with an increased range of administrative and management functions they are required to undertake. Hours spent in the office means less time spent with people. Smart leaders need to find ways of rebalancing their priorities.

NEW JOB ROLES

Finally partnership working invites us to rethink the range of support roles that are provided to meet the new aspirations and styles of working. At a minimum this may mean expanding job descriptions of paid supporters so that partnership working is seen as a key feature of the job with training and mentoring offered to develop the staff's skills in this aspect of their role. Similarly the person specification for jobs will look for people who have the personal qualities suited to working in conjunction with others and of having the connections within their local communities to facilitate links.

When there are a number of supporters within the one service, one can be designated as the named supporter (sometimes called a key-worker). The idea is that this person can act as a point of contact with other supporters such as family members or staff in another agency. It helps if the nominated supporter has a particular affinity with the person they support. The named supporter is not expected to be the sole supporter but rather their role is to ensure that relevant information is collated and passed within the support team as well as liaising with others outside of the team. This should ensure better co-ordination of supporter's efforts especially those working with groups of people[106].

Another strategy services can use is to create a new type of support worker whose prime responsibility is to build partnerships among people and organisations (see Box)[107]. These posts have various titles and ways of working but one thing they have in common. Of necessity this staff member is not located within a service but rather he or she spends most of their working time in community settings.

Lorna's job

My post is 'community coordinator' and it's my ideal job. I've lived in the town all my life and been involved in voluntary work with various organisations. I'd enjoyed being a social worker but lately all the form filling became too much for me. But I had gotten to know the various services that are available in our town. Now I use my connections to link people in with local activities and groups.

The old saying is true – it's who you know, not what you know, that important. That's why I belong to lots of different community groups for you never know when the contacts will come in handy. If they can't help you themselves, they often put you in touch with someone who can.

A third approach is for supporters to play multiple roles. For example, a family supporter may also be employed in services, help as a volunteer in the local Gateway Club and be a friend to other family carers. Likewise a staff member who belongs to a local drama group may become a community supporter to other people and a particular friend to a person with whom he previously worked.

These multiple support roles are already happening. Many staff and volunteers mention a family member as a reason for why they chose to apply for jobs in services. Community supporters may become paid workers or develop close friendships with some families or people in need of support.

Our experience is that these different relationships benefit everyone and they can contribute greatly to partnership working.

- It lets supporters experience a different perspective. They can feel what it's like to be in another place. It gives them a wider view of what's happening beyond their 'day-to-day' work.
- It gives supporters access to a wider range of people who can support them and the people they are supporting. These social networks can prevent feelings of isolation and despondency.
- It forms 'natural' bridges between groups of supporters that otherwise may be disconnected. Human society relies on personal relationships to bring people together and to cross the divides that can separate us.

We realise that supporters can't be forced to take on other roles, many are fully stretched already. But some supporters are prepared to branch out and help others. The reward is often a richer but busier life.

In case we have painted too daunting a picture of what supporters are expected to do, we end with two consolations. People grow naturally into the varied contributions to partnerships that we have described in this chapter just as they do in their personal life. And second, their core concern must remain their relationship with the person they support; all else is building on that.

BALANCING RISKS AND OPPORTUNITIES

In his autobiography, Christopher Nolan[108] paints a wonderful picture of the support he received from his family. Born with profound physical disabilities he was totally dependent on his parents and sister. He recalls a family holiday in the West of Ireland when they went swimming in the Atlantic Ocean. In his book he refers to himself as Joseph.

> All hands joined forces to help Joseph swim and float in the warm currents. They floated him with them as they moved out to sea: he glowed with pleasure as he skimmed along for he felt totally relaxed and safe in their hands and through their efforts he sampled the joys of the able-bodied (p. 104).

The image of his frail body being floated in the Atlantic Ocean captures well the exciting opportunities that supporters can create for people that otherwise they would be denied. The benefits were many – notice the words used to describe the experience: "glowed, pleasure, relaxed, safe, joys".

And yet, the family were taking a risk: indeed some may even describe the whole escapade as foolhardy. What if a huge wave suddenly swamped them? What if Joseph took a 'turn'? What if his father had a heart attack? What if his mother sprained her back? What if …what if … what if … The list could go on and on!

But how real were the risks they faced? No doubt the family judged it safe, as it's unlikely they would knowingly put their own lives or that of Joseph at stake. The seas were calm, his father was fit and healthy, there were three of them to look after Joseph, all were strong swimmers, and they were well practiced as sea-swimming was something they had done as a family since the children were small. When these considerations were placed against the possible risks, albeit unconsciously, the family decided to take the opportunity of having fun together!

RISK AVERSIVE SERVICES

Supporters who are not family members may not enjoy such freedoms: especially those who are in paid employment. Service agencies today are very concerned about the health and safety of their staff, the risk of harm to people using their services and the possibility of being sued for negligence[109]. Likewise regulation authorities take a dim view of vulnerable people being placed at risk and may insist that precautions are put in place to prevent anything untoward happening. This could mean, among others things, having a hoist available so that paid supporters do not harm themselves in lifting Joseph into the water and ensuring that a life-guard is present. In addition everyone would probably have to wear life jackets. If these conditions cannot be met, then the activity will not proceed – despite the wishes of the person – and certainly not on the spur of the moment. The risks are perceived to outweigh the benefits that the opportunity offers to the person.

Finding the balance between risks and opportunities pervades all human endeavours although we may not consciously think in these terms. Leaving your home to go to work for example, brings with it certain risks – small though they be, especially when you take sensible precautions and avoid unnecessary dangers.

However when you are taking risks on behalf of a person deemed to be vulnerable, then higher standards are expected to apply for the reasons described above. But this should not mean dealing with risk through avoiding the activity. Rather the issue is one of managing the risk – reducing the likelihood of ill effects arising. Implicitly this means accepting that risk can never be totally eliminated. If we are so pre-occupied with preventing any form of danger then the person would be wrapped so much in cotton wool that they are smothered. Conversely if we discount risks as improbable, we may expose the person to unnecessary dangers. We would then be failing in our 'duty-to-care' for them and our own well-being.

It is fine balancing act for supporters to determine what is a *reasonable* risk. Not surprisingly this can be a common area of disagreement among supporters, family carers and even between supporters and the people they support. The result is frequently a lot more talking is done with decisions being put off ... and off!

In modern services, prescribed procedures and risk assessments can dominate decision-making[110]. Rightful concerns about people's vulnerability to abuse – physical, sexual, social or financial abuse – have resulted in new regulations that have tightened up checking procedures for people recruited to services either as staff or as volunteers. Likewise health and safety concerns prohibit certain activities from taking place unless safeguards are in place; as much to protect supporters sometimes as the people they support. If these safeguards are prohibitively expensive, then the activity cannot happen. An over concern with risk permeates much current of modern service delivery, and indeed in many elements of society more generally, with the consequence that the lives of people we support are constrained and impoverished.

FINDING A BALANCE

A sense of balance is required from supporters in assessing and managing risks[111]. This is readily attainable with supportive leadership and when supporters work together in partnerships with each other and with the people they support[112]. Think again of Joseph and his family. In our experience three strategies will guide you through the process of balancing risks and opportunities (which admittedly is not always easy or straightforward) and give you the courage to act.

First, focus on the individual person in need of support. There is a tendency to base risk assessments on groups of people – for instance, those labelled as 'disabled'; 'elderly' or 'mentally confused'. But this is very unfair on individuals as any group label covers a diversity of capabilities. A key issue we will stress is the individual's own capacity to understand and to manage risks.

Second, supporters must have a shared understanding of the outcomes a person wants from life and any particular courses of action. This will ensure that we work towards their best interests.

Third, a network of friends and supporters provide a safety net and protection against potential risks and harm. These can be mobilised to look out for the person. People who are isolated and friendless are at much greater risk of being taken advantage of.

The time and effort involved in building this foundation pays dividends in balancing risks and opportunities.

LEARNING FROM EXPERIENCE

Assessing risks is all about predicting what *might* happen. Predicting the future is not easy as any betting man or women will tell you. Yet when it comes to vulnerable people, there's a common perception that we have to get it right all of the time; there's no room for any mistakes. If there are slip-ups then somebody is to blame and frequently the finger is pointed at the supporters who let it happen. Here are some examples.

> The service had a policy that no resident can leave a group home unless accompanied by a member of staff. In response to pressure from residents, the managers and staff team agreed to change it but only after much debate and argument. A few months later a resident was knocked down and seriously injured near the home. The local newspaper called for an enquiry into mis-management of the home. The staff team reversed their decision despite the residents' wishes.

Were the staff of the home really to blame? Allowing people to live more independent lives means them taking on greater risks yet as supporters we must ensure that people are adequately prepared to do so. People have to learn to manage risks. If the staff took all reasonable precautions and an accident does occur; then fresh assessments of risks should be undertaken but this has to be done with each person. Denying some residents an opportunity to do what they are able to do ignores their individuality and potentially weakens their self-confidence.

> Josie wanted to attend yoga classes at the local college. Her key-worker found out the times and costs. She thought it best to phone the yoga teacher in advance and explain a little of Josie's needs. But when the teacher heard that Josie had special needs, she said her insurance wouldn't cover her if anything went wrong. Josie would need to be accompanied at all times. For a few weeks, this was possible but staff shortages meant that no one could go with Josie to College so she had to drop out.

This time the reason given was lack of insurance cover – or was it? Sometimes an excuse is invented to cover other reasons for not taking a risk. A better strategy may have been for Josie to turn up with a supporter who stayed with her for a couple of weeks so that the tutor and the others could see that she would pose little risk. They would get to know Josie as a person rather than as a label – a person with special needs. Sadly though insurance companies don't often work like this. They apply blanket sanctions which can be very unfair to individuals.

> Tim can be physically boisterous. He had been going to the same family for overnight breaks for many years. On the last visit, he appeared to sexually assault one of the children and the placement was immediately discontinued by the social worker when informed by the host family. His parents think it was a misunderstanding and the host family are willing to give Tim another chance but the service does not want to risk a repetition and will not try to reactivate the placement.

Do we know what actually happened between Tim and the child? People have come to different conclusions and a decision has been made by social workers that might be unfair on Tim and his family. A careful investigation needs to be conducted to find out the facts and learn lessons from it. For example, Tim may need to know when his behaviour is inappropriate and safeguards are put in place to help him and protect others. In some ways this is a more difficult path for the social workers to follow but taking the easier option of withdrawing a service is no help to Tim or his family.

In these stories, some of the incidents could have been foreseen and been managed better, other times the events happen by accident as can be the case in our own lives. The danger is that if we try to eliminate all risks – which insurance companies for example would like us to do – then many opportunities are lost to the person we are supporting. They don't go to the shops alone, they can't enrol for Yoga classes or they are stopped from staying with other families.

Of course these prohibitions are done with the best of intentions but the safe option is not without its costs. People are denied valued experiences; prevented from acquiring new skills and barred from taking responsibility. Supporters too may suffer. They are forced back into 'controlling' people's lives; they may feel guilty about letting the person down and start to feel demoralised about ever changing the attitudes and practices of service systems.

GUIDING PRINCIPLES IN BALANCING RISKS

How then might supporters become better predictors of risks and manage them in such a way that the person we are supporting benefits? There are five principles we need to keep in mind.

Person-centred

Each risk assessment has to be done anew with each individual[113]. For example, you cannot presume that all the people living in houses with 24-hour support staff are not able to go to the local pub unaccompanied. While this may be true for certain people in the group home, it may not necessarily true for others.

This person-centred principle challenges service rules or practices that prohibit all people from certain activities. This may be convenient and reassuring for managers but is probably not in the person's interests and may well infringe their rights. Rather person-centredness requires detailed knowledge of the individuals so that we can assess their likely reactions should risks arise. This means knowing a person's story in some detail so that we can build up a picture of their strengths and weaknesses. We have to gain an insight into their understandings and emotions. We need to know about their past behaviours as these are likely to predict how they will react in future. All of this information comes best from the person and from those supporters who spend most time with him or her.

Planning

All our risk assessments have to be rooted in the overall support plan that has been developed for, and hopefully *with* the person. This describes the outcomes we are aiming to achieve and provides the rationale for our decisions that may expose the person to reasonable risks. Moreover the plan places the focus on the positive benefits that will accrue to the person from the outcomes rather than a negative focus on dangers; real though they may be!

This leads on to a more detailed appraisal of the kinds of risks that might arise during the specified activity and the likelihood of their occurring. Past experience can be drawn upon preferably based on actual instances that have arisen in the past the person or others like him or her. Ways of minimising the risks can also be planned. Again past experience is a good teacher as is a creative mind.

Involvement of the person

Our end goal is for people we support to understand and manage risks for themselves, and not depend on us to do it for them. Thus from the outset we must involve them in the process of assessing risks. We need to listen and respect their viewpoint. Admittedly this is not always easy as people may well have different views than we do and they may not want to hear any other viewpoint to theirs. However these disputes are a vital part of developing greater independence and encouraging self-reliance. Remember as a teenager how you negotiated with your parents to be allowed to take 'risks'? So too, as supporters we need to be prepared to engage with the people we support in deciding what are acceptable risks.

> **Linda's story**
> All I wanted was a cigarette. I asked this man for a ciggie outside the pub. He said come in for a drink. I did. Then he put his arms around me and tried to kiss me. I pushed him away and got out quick. I ran home, all nervy and 'fraid. I cried and cried. That night the staff had a meeting with me. We agreed that I could still go into town but I was not to ask men I don't know for cigarettes. I was to take the mobile with me and call them if I was scared. Just before I leave the house, I'd have a smoke and I'd get another one when I came home. But they're finding out about me wearing some patches for protection against smoking because they tell me it's bad for me".

This principle of involvement challenges the presumption that people are incapable of understanding dangers and protecting themselves from risk. Rather we have to assist them to acquire this capacity; a topic we will come back to later.

A second important reason for involving the person is because some people may lack the self-confidence to take on new challenges. They will not risk going it alone or tackling anything new. Here the supporter may have to find ways of instilling some risk into people's lives. If they manage these without mishap, the chances are their confidence and self-esteem will grow, and in turn they will be more eager to accept further risks. Of course, similar strategies may have to be deployed to persuade supporters who hold different viewpoints. Those who are eager to avoid risks may be won over as the person demonstrates that they can cope.

The outcomes of these debates need to be written down so that we don't forget the decisions taken. A visual summary might be prepared of the dangers and of how they can be avoided; especially to remind the person in need of support.

We realise that some people cannot take part in discussions of this sort but even so we suggest that they should be physically present when decisions that affect them personally are being taken. They might be accompanied by an advocate who can speak on their behalf, especially when their rights and freedoms are being constrained (see Chapter 2).

Participation of all supporters

Ideally all the main supporters of a person should contribute to the risk assessment so that they have a mutual understanding of the reasons underpinning it. This includes all the members of the staff team working in the same service with the person. Family supporters should also be involved or those in other services or community settings as appropriate, although issues of confidentiality will have a bearing on this. Often this consultation can be done within the context of a person-centred planning meeting or for more contentious issues through a specially convened meeting. It may be necessary for a written statement about the decision reached to be signed and dated by all the supporters who were consulted in its preparation. This can be added to the person's plan.

With less contentious decisions, consultations may be done by speaking personally to the supporters involved or by telephoning them.

Review your decisions

Any decision we make needs to be reviewed so that we can learn to make better judgements in the future. These reviews are just as vital when things are going well and not only when things go wrong. Of course the review will be based on the four principles we have just described: the review needs to be a shared learning experience particularly for the person we are supporting. The review should help you to pinpoint which of your judgements were confirmed and those that were mistaken. You can then revise your risk management strategy and revisit your judgements: a topic to which we now turn.

BALANCED JUDGEMENTS

Having outlined the process, how can we arrive at a judgement about risk? Four aspects have to be balanced against one another as per the framework in the following Figure.

Figure: Factors influencing decisions about risks

This is not an exact science and we have to do the best with the evidence that is available to us at that time of coming to a decision. We also need to keep a sense of perspective and apply what some might call 'common-sense'. We cannot plan for every eventuality, as some risks are highly unlikely to occur.

Capacity

Capacity is a legal term. It refers to a person's ability to make decisions based on an understanding of the risks involved and free from coercion by others. People in need of support are often presumed to lack the 'mental capacity' to make decisions for themselves largely because they are deemed unable to "guard themselves against common dangers or exploitation"[114]. Likewise, the law states that children under specified ages are not capable of making certain decisions. Also people with mental illness or an intellectual disability can be judged as lacking capacity.

However modern thinking[115] has moved away from making blanket presumptions about an adult person's capacity to make decisions for themselves because of a disability. Rather the focus is on making the judgement about their capacity in relation to specific individuals and the activity or actions around which a decision has to be made. This means that one person may be judged to have the capacity to decide about learning to drive a car whereas another person would not. However because we decide the person has the capacity to drive a car does not automatically mean he has the capacity to make decisions about getting married, for example. A new judgement would be needed on this issue.

Lawyers talk about certain 'tests' being applied in making an assessment of a person's capacity to decide. But they do not give absolute answers. Rather they help us to arrive at a judgement about the likelihood of the person of being capable to make decisions. The following are some of the 'tests' commonly used in assessing a person's capacity.

– Does the person understand the information relevant to the decision?

– Can the person retain the information and remember it?

– Can the person weigh up the reasonably foreseeable consequences of deciding one way or the other, or of failing to make any decisions?

– Can the person communicate his decision either verbally, by sign language or any other means?

Assessments of capacity have to be undertaken by people who know the person well and they are best done as a team effort drawing on all the evidence that is available at the time. These discussions will also help to identify the gaps in the person's knowledge and understanding which future support plans can address. Thus conclusions about a person's capacity to be involved in decision-making are rarely black-and-white and even when they are, the decisions need to be reviewed as circumstances and people change.

Ali was a keen supporter of Manchester United. He talked often of travelling from Ireland to see them play. His support staff jollied him along thinking it could never happen. When Tom joined the team as a new staff member he wondered why not go for it? He discussed with Ali how much it would cost – did he have other plans for spending his money? He checked out what Ali knew about flying – had he done it before? He knew Ali had been to local football matches but how did he feel about being in crowds? Ali agreed that Tom could check out what others felt about him travelling to Manchester with Tom to see the match.

The issue of capacity must be primary in all our decision-making. If a person is judged to lack capacity with regard to making decisions about a particular activity, then our duty-of-care means we must not expose him or her to unnecessary risk despite what the person may say. For instance she cannot be allowed to learn to drive or he will not be able to get married. This is because the person does not fully understand the risks involved and is unable to guard themselves against the dangers to self and others inherent in them. But this does NOT mean that they should be stopped from doing related activities, such as having a girlfriend, as they could be judged to have the capacity to decide on these.

However a more common scenario in our experience is when people clearly have the capacity to decide and yet they are still prevented from doing what they want to do. There may be good reasons for this but the other three factors in the framework will help to tease them out if this is so.

Competence

A question is this: does the person have the necessary competence to undertake the activity or action proposed? For instance, if we don't know how to swim, it is bigger risk for us to go out in a sailing boat than if we can swim! Hence our assessments of a person's competence are an important factor in making judgements of risk.

Yet this is not always straightforward. The competence to undertake an activity is often a combination of different skills and personal qualities. For example, to go to the local shops unaccompanied, a person will need to know how to cross the road safely; to remember the directions to the shop and back home again; and be able to make purchases when they get there. Moreover the person may be capable of doing these tasks but lacks confidence in doing them, or he may be fearful of things going wrong and so on.

Analysing activities in this way encourages us to consider the person's abilities as well as their disabilities. It reminds us of specific skills that the person may need to learn and helps us assess how realistic it is for the person to acquire new skills. Of course the activity selected – going to the shops alone – may be a very good way of developing their skills.

Tom and Ali drew up a list of all the money they were likely to spend for the proposed trip to Manchester. They devised a savings plan to cover the costs and checked to see that Ali kept to it. When they next went to a local match, Tom observed how Ali managed when they were in the ground – finding their seats, going to the toilet, buying drinks – and his reactions when among crowds.

Outcomes

What are the likely outcomes of the person participating in the chosen activity? If the possible negative outcomes of an activity are focussed on, this too will increase perceptions of risk. Thus if we think about leaving the person on their own at home, bringing with it the risk of them falling downstairs, opening the door to strangers or flooding the place – we will be less inclined to it. Conversely an activity can be seen to have positive outcomes for the person – it builds their self-confidence; gives them privacy and the freedom to do what they want. This may cause us to think again about how likely is it really for the person is to have an accident when home alone. We can consider the actions we can take to avoid it happening.

We make these sort of 'cost-benefit' analyses of risks all the time in our own lives and parents do the same for their children. *"I'd love to go swimming in the sea but I might catch a chill, get stung by a jelly-fish or swept off-shore and drown."* If we judge that the costs outweigh the benefits, we play safe and don't even try the activity and will happily forego the benefits. Which in fact is a cost in itself. The solution to this dilemma lies in the fourth element in the framework.

> When Tom first brought up at the staff meeting the idea of Ali going to Manchester it had a mixed response. Some reported how Ali can be panicked by crowds, how he liked his routine and would be anxious staying in hotels, while others stated that he couldn't afford it! When Tom steered the discussion towards potential benefits, people did admit that Ali would enjoy it, he'll have something to boast about and it would give him something to look forward to.

Conditions

The probability of negative outcomes arising can be reduced by the conditions under which the activity is performed. For example, the risk of dangers from using public transport will be reduced if the person is accompanied by friends or a supporter, or if they have a mobile phone to call for help should they get lost. The conditions under which the activity occurs may include the time the activity occurs, the people to be present, as well as the preparations and precautions that should be in place. The conditions can also take account of the person's competence, personal disposition and particular behaviours.

> Tom drew up a plan for the trip. He and Ali would have their mobile phones with them at all times. They practiced calling each other. They took a trip out to the airport to familiarise Ali with the check-in routine. Tom talked to a friend who had been to Manchester United's ground and got directions to

their allocated seats which were on an aisle for easy access. They planned to leave before the match was over, to avoid the crowds.

The result is a support plan in risk management tailored to that individual. It may start with a strong emphasis on supervision but as the person demonstrates his or her competence, this can be gradually reduced so that the person takes more responsibility. Equally if the person takes unnecessary risks or dangers increase then we may need to increase our supervision and support. That's why we listed the undertaking of regular reviews as a fifth principle in managing risk.

Finally, support plans and changes to them should not be decided by individual supporters. Their judgements need to be checked out by at least one other person as an added safeguard for both themselves and the person they support.

Implementing the framework

Describing a framework for decision-making about risk is easy; implementing it is harder. This is especially so within a service philosophy that places particular emphasis on care and protection for vulnerable people[116]. Many families espouse a similar ethos for their relatives, as do many of our professional services. Indeed increased regulation and the threat of litigation have resulted in services becoming more reluctant to take risks. This state of affairs will continue and may even worsen, if we do not identify means of counteracting these trends. We have identified some of the means for doing this already including advocacy for or by the person, taking a person-centred approach, ensuring partnership working and that there is effective leadership. To this list can be added:

Experience: We can draw upon the learning that we have gained with other people in similar situations or with the person as they have embarked on the chosen activity. This learning needs to be shared with others so that their opinions are based on the most up-to-date information.

Support Networks: Has the person the friends and social networks that will provide the additional supports that may be required to provide an additional safety net?

Results: We need to evaluate the results that have been observed – both positive and negative – of the actions taken. This will help to readjust the supports we make available.

Even with all these elements underpinning the framework, certain decisions can be especially challenging such as those around sexual behaviour, marriage and having children, as explored in Chapter 5[117]. Or those that expose the person to potential exploitation and abuse, such as the choice of friends who may take advantage of the individual. These may raise questions of morality, right and wrong behaviours. Is it OK to have sex outside of marriage or for people to have a gay relationship? Should people be allowed to spend their money getting drunk or buying pornographic magazines?

There are no ready-made answers to these dilemmas. Most parents encounter them as their children mature into adulthood and many will feel that they never handled them particularly well. This analogy is a reminder of the need for the people we support to be rooted into communities so that they are exposed to moral codes that will guide their behaviours and relationships.

However supporters need to beware of imposing their personal morality on the people they support and likewise, challenge other supporters if they act unilaterally in this way. That's another reason why decisions should be taken in consultation with other supporters. Our goal is always to support people to make their own decisions.

Risks and opportunities are not opposites but part of the same dynamic we call life. For each person, at a point in life and at a moment in time, the opportunities will wax and wane, just as the risks will come and go. There are no absolutes to which we can anchor. Rather like Christopher Nolan and his family, we have to continually judge when it is safe to venture forth so that our folk too can *"sample the joys of the able-bodied"*.

FINDING FULFILMENT

When you have cherished a wish and have charged me with its fulfilment, have I ever replied, 'It is impossible'?

Alexandre Dumas

In this book we have looked at what it means to share our lives as equals with people in need of particular supports. We gathered together some of the elements that create a true and valuing image of those we support, based on the testimony of observers and on what people have to say for themselves. We wrote in the tradition of positive psychology where the focus is on people's capabilities and strengths rather than disabilities and pathology.

Mutual relationships and community were focussed on as they are primary human needs that all of us have. We made suggestions as to how these needs are to be understood and realised with the people we support, and how they can play their role in relationship and community building, if given a chance.

Throughout, the crucial role of supporters was highlighted, whether families, community supporters or paid supporters, and we attended to what they gain as much as to what they can give in supporting others. We urged the building of support networks, and discussed the kind of culture that a service needs in order to embrace and realise the values we propose.

We are excited by the vision presented and realise that we are only articulating what many people already know and practice. The deep fulfilment to be found in working in this way is something we have experienced ourselves for many years, and we know it is available to anybody who takes a valuing approach to people in need of support. We also believe that their fulfilment depends on being related to and appreciated in this way.

But our vision is not without its fears and we cannot afford to be naive. Currently we are living in a relatively benign era with respect to the social acceptance of diversity. Societies have known such positive phases before, but history shows they subsequently deteriorated into the most appalling mistreatment and denigration of people who were perceived as different and inferior. It helps nobody if we pretend that such things could never happen again.

So, in this final chapter we do four things. We explore the conditions for achieving a fulfilled life with a particular focus on the spiritual aspects of our humanity. We list the many hopeful signs that point towards fulfilment for those we support and for their supporters. Yet we note the signs that should make us fearful, in the hope that awareness of the dangers will sharpen vigilance and commitment. And we highlight what is essential as we move together into an uncharted future.

THE HOPE OF FULFILMENT

As outlined in this book, and like everybody else, the people we support feel fulfilled when they have achieved their desires, particularly the desire for meaningful personal relationships and a sense of belonging wherever they live. Supporters, in turn, find fulfilment in their relationships with them and in the contentment they feel from helping them achieve their desires. Now we take the argument one stage further and examine the essence of the humanity that we share and in particular what is sometimes called the spiritual dimension to our lives.

Services and their personnel often underestimate the role they can and should play in affirming the human spirit of those they support. That may be because spirituality has been equated with the formal practices of various religious traditions, usually on days and in settings set aside for that purpose. Many service supporters mistakenly see it as lying outside their role.

In fairness, it must be said that service supporters are not alone in the neglect of spirituality. Until relatively recently, little attention was given by anybody to the spiritual development of the people we support. This is slowly being addressed now, particularly through the action research conducted by people such as John Swinton[118], Chris Hatton[119] and their colleagues. Their findings are a close fit with the major themes of this book, particularly regarding the centrality of relationships and community in the growth and expression of a person's spirit. Supporters cannot neglect this aspect of people's lives.

> Recognising and enabling the spiritual needs of people with a learning disability is not an option, but a vital dimension of caring and support practices which has significant legal as well as moral implications. The question is not, "Is spirituality relevant?" but rather, "What are the best ways in which carers and

support workers can be enabled to understand and effectively incorporate this dimension of their client's experience into their day to day practice?"

Swinton (2002)

UNDERSTANDING SPIRITUALITY

Rather than being something esoteric and intangible, Swinton defines spirituality as that aspect of our existence that gives it 'humanness.' It gives meaning and direction to a person's life by striving to answer fundamental questions about what we are as human beings, why we are here, and what we can and should become. It also encompasses our concern for love and for relationships, for beauty and harmony, for awe and wonder.

For some, spirituality need not include any religion at all, while for others religion may be central to their spirituality. All religions are based on a degree of shared history and belief, on ritual, symbolism and often prayer. Equally, a belief in a divine Being might be central to a person's religious experience without any need for the structures and creed of an established religion.

Spirituality is fundamentally part of humanity, and formal religion is just one important means of seeking to understand and fulfil spiritual needs. Swinton quotes the Dalai Lama on the distinction between the two (p. 5).

> Spirituality I take to be concerned with those qualities of the human spirit – such as love and compassion, patience, tolerance, forgiveness, contentment, a sense of responsibility, a sense of harmony – which bring happiness to both self and others. While ritual and prayer, along with the questions of nirvana and salvation, are directly connected with religious faith, these inner qualities need not be, however. There is thus no reason why the individual should not develop them, even to a high degree, without recourse to any religious or metaphysical belief system. This is why I sometimes say that religion is something we can perhaps do without. What we cannot do without are these basic spiritual qualities.

This separation of religion and spirituality is important, because it means that a person can be supported to grow spiritually without the supporter needing to understand or share a particular religious tradition. Feeling ill equipped or untrained in this area need not inhibit a supporter in appreciating the spiritual.

Indeed it is impossible to expect supporters to become experts in all the religions they might encounter amongst people with learning disabilities. It is far more important for supporters to know how to **listen** to a person to find out how they understand their faith and what it means to them, than to apply a textbook knowledge of religion that might not fit the person at all. Supporters will then learn about the person's faith in a way that is relevant to the person and that will help them to support the person in their religious interests[120].

Basing our contributions on what we learn by listening to what people themselves want, also addresses supporters' fears that they may be adding to pressure on people to attend religious activities against their will or to follow particular beliefs and practices.

Hence affirming people's spirituality is not just a role for religious professionals then, but is for all who seek to offer holistic care and support. Indeed research has shown a positive correlation between spirituality and physical and mental well-being, and that belief systems have an important role in helping people understand and cope with the complexities of life[121]. In addition, human support and opportunities for friendship can flow from shared spiritual and religious activities.

ENABLING THE GROWTH OF THE HUMAN SPIRIT

In considering how to support a person's spiritual growth, it is necessary to understand something more about spirituality. This includes realising that:

- relationships are central in building a person's spiritual life;
- spiritual knowledge can occur intuitively as well as intellectually;
- sensory experiences enhance an appreciation of the spiritual;
- community can creates the space in which people can express and fulfil a spiritual life;
- formal worship can be nurturing for people, and,
- the person we support can be a spiritual teacher for others.

Relationships and spirituality

> It is only as we enter into meaningful relationships with others and find ourselves loved and affirmed, that we can begin to understand what it means to care and accept that we are worthy of being loved and cared for.... Friendship is a primary spiritual relationship which can be invaluable for fulfilling the spiritual needs of people with learning disabilities.
>
> **Swinton 2001**

Relationships are central to our spirituality. They are the means through which love, hope, affirmation and commitment are expressed. Caring and love is experienced not just through words, but also through eye contact, touch, and tone of voice – all additionally relevant to people limited or lacking in language.

Those we support may have a poor understanding of historical time. Many cannot interpret the past, only the present. What matters is what is happening right now, generally as expressed through others and their interactions. This means that there can be spiritual nourishment and affirmation in the simplest acts of each day. The supporter often offers this without conscious effort. At other times, careful preparation is needed, in order to be able to look with a consistent love on the other person[122].

Spirituality can be known intuitively as well as intellectually

A reason sometimes given for not taking seriously the spiritual life of people with intellectual disabilities, is that they cannot understand enough about abstract concepts such as a divine Being and religion to be a true participant. Yet it is also agreed that even the greatest brain in the world cannot gain an intellectual understanding of a Divinity that is totally 'spirit.'

As we saw above, spirituality relates to specific ways of being in the world that cannot be understood through intellect and reason alone, yet it expresses the deepest longing of the human heart. Hence the person who is intellectually disabled is equally capable of encountering the spiritual as is anybody else.

As Harrington notes, faith education is not "a transmission of knowledge but is essentially a call to relate, which is done not intellectually but affectively." She goes on to note that the quality of affectivity is determined by the quality of relationships, and can also be enhanced by the use of the senses.

Sense experiences enhance an appreciation of the spiritual

The experience of being looked upon and treated with love and respect, allows the person to gain an intuitive knowledge of spiritual qualities. Such experiences can be enhanced by the senses. Being out in the beauty of the countryside or by the sea; having quiet times to a background of peaceful music; the rich colours and perfume of flowers; the use of incense or the smell of baking; the quality and form of light; the welcoming warmth of a place; the pleasure of a nice meal – all these things help people enter into an awareness of the spiritual.

Celebrating together is one of life's highlights and an essential aspect of being human. We all need the lift that such occasions can bring. Our daily life often brings its own weariness. We need something beyond these limitations. This can be found in the sharing of simple everyday meals as well as on special occasions, as noted by Sue Mosteller[123] from her years of living in l'Arche.

> The meals themselves are a time of utmost importance for the bodily nourishment and for all it signifies. Perhaps here, at the table our strongest experience is the taste of our solidarity. The stories, the bantering, the remarks about the cooking, the serving and passing of the food, the arguments, the broken diets and the sharing of the last piece of cake, all enter the same message into my hungry heart, the message that I belong to this people and I am acceptable, as I am here: that this is my home.

A sensitive supporter will find similar opportunities to create affective and sensual moments that can help connect people to one another at a deeper emotional level.

Community creates the living space for spirituality

Because relationship with others is so central to spirituality, the experience of community greatly enhances a person's spiritual life. Healthy communities offer safe spaces within which friendships can develop and be sustained.

Faith communities can be particularly supportive to people's spiritual life. They should all be places where people find acceptance and are valued, and there are great gains for all members where this happens.

Des was really struggling. He was getting into trouble with the law and was difficult to work with. Since his Mum passed away, he was not receiving the care he needed from either his family or his local service. Without support his life became chaotic; he neglected his appearance and general self-care. It was clear that Des was becoming depressed and more and more a loner.

Kieran, the pastoral worker, invited Des on four 'retreat weekends' in a row, spread over a couple of months, with a companion each time. At first Des was closed and silent, but gradually he emerged from his shell. He met new friends, felt held by the community, and was touched by the worship services and the general atmosphere of spiritual attentiveness.

The theme of the final weekend was 'Behold, I make all things new.' At the end, Des said, "coming here has made me a new man." It became possible for Kieran to link him into other activities, including a community drama group where Des was able to tell his own story through participation in various group activities. He still struggles from time to time, but he has found a new security and a new base to which to return when life becomes difficult.

Sadly, not all faith communities are as open to members who need support. Some may be as excluding as the rest of society. Accordingly, people may need support when knocking on the door of the religion that is their tradition, or which now attracts them as independent adults[124]. The supporter can help in a variety of ways:

– If asked, accompanying people when initially attending their religious communities.

– Speaking of the gifts of an individual, so that the value they bring to the faith community can be recognised and appreciated.

– Inviting some community members, including its leaders, to visit people at home or in shared activities.

– Seeking a member of the community who would be willing to become part of a person's circle of support.

Formal worship can nurture people

Formal worship gathers people together to give expression to their common beliefs as a faith community. It ritualises human experience, focussing on major themes such as love and belonging, hurt and forgiveness, despair and hope, life and death, in the context of a loving Divine Being.

Some people love to attend the rituals that are part of the community worship of their own religious tradition.

Colm goes to his local church almost every evening of the week. He needs regularity in life and the ritual seems to give him comfort. He gets to the church early, and can be heard talking to himself out loud regarding whatever is on his mind. Nobody minds as he is well accepted by the small group that gathers there with him. But as soon as the ritual begins, Colm becomes calm, joining in all the prayers and taking communion. He clearly loves the liturgy, and the only time he interjects is if the priest does something that Colm thought was not a correct part of the liturgy!

The communities of Faith and Light are specifically built around people who need support, their families and friends. It is an ecumenical movement that includes members from different Christian traditions as well as people who don't attend church at all. There are now thousands of members of Faith and Light communities worldwide, with meetings designed so that all can participate equally in worship and contemplation.

> We try to make our worship as visual and as participatory as possible. We often use gestures and signing with our hands in our prayers and in our singing. Sometimes we incorporate into our worship some simple activity where everybody contributes something.... After our worship we share news, remember people's birthdays, take part in a raffle and then conclude our time together with a shared meal. Everybody is encouraged to bring some food to share so there's usually a great pile of sandwiches, sausage rolls and cakes which all disappear very quickly[125].

The person as spiritual teacher

Finally as in all other areas, the people we support can make a major contribution to the development of a spiritual life, not only for themselves but also for others. They too possess the qualities of the human spirit listed earlier by the Dalai Lama 'such as love and compassion, patience, tolerance, forgiveness, contentment, a sense of responsibility, a sense of harmony – which bring happiness to both self and others.' But this will only happen only to the degree that others are open to experiencing their gifts and in allowing the person to challenge and transform them. This brings us back to where we started at the outset of this book.

In sum, there is good reason to hope that more people will be given the chance to lead fulfilled lives if enough energy goes into creating the opportunities they need for building relationships and community. But achieving this asks of their supporters a change of heart, a change of mind, and a change of spirit. In so doing, the gains are as great for the supporters as for the people they support.

A CHANGE OF HEART

We hope that what you have read in this book may heighten or even change how you feel about the people you support and your role in meeting their needs. But we also want you to think and feel differently about yourself, and we suggest some ideas that we believe can inspire and empower supporters when they feel overwhelmed and disheartened.

Life is getting better

Medical science, therapeutic advances and educational interventions have markedly reduced the impact of disabilities on people's lives and the facilities for many have greatly improved and continue to do so; although sad to say they are not always readily available to everyone who could benefit from them. Nonetheless, we are privileged to be living at times when hope is more than a pipe-dream. This spirit of optimism needs to pervade all our endeavours. It is a powerful antidote when inevitably feelings of despair are encountered. We need to practice seeing the glass as half full rather than half empty.

People can change

Every one of us has the potential to become more than who we are at this moment in time. Without this belief, we would not apply for new jobs, enter new relationships or try new leisure pursuits. It motivates us to achieve and helps us to become the person we aspire to be. The same is true of the people we support. We need to tune into their hopes and aspirations and believe that change is possible albeit at a slower pace. Likewise, a belief in the potential for change can sustain us as we seek to encourage various individuals and communities to share their lives with those we support.

Goodwill still exists

Although modern society has become more impersonal, people of goodwill can be found in every community. Their willingness to be involved may vary, but unless they are invited they will not put themselves forward. We need to be better at identifying the contributions that our fellow citizens can make and find ways of encouraging their participation. Older teenagers are particularly important, not least because they are the service workforce of the future.

I can do it!

Have faith in yourself. Do not compare yourself to others whom you think more knowledgeable, more able, more motivated than you. You are committed to supporting a particular individual or group, and it is in your grasp to do the job that needs to be done at this moment in time. So think about your talents, your skills, your achievements and ask why not me?

A CHANGE OF MIND

A change of mind is also needed but it isn't always easy to make. We tend to go along with how things have been done rather than expend the effort or take the risks involved in changing. In recent decades we've had a big change of mind about how best to assist people who have been labelled as 'disabled'. This has not happened suddenly and in many ways it is still incomplete, but among the main changes it brings are the following:

People don't need to be in special centres

We've changed our mind about how to deliver services to people. The days of bringing people together into large specialist centres are numbered. Admittedly they had some advantages but these were mainly in terms of management and staffing. The biggest drawback for the people using these facilities was their lack of control over their own lives, their social isolation, and the lack of access to the opportunities enjoyed by their fellow-citizens. The solution was self-evident but it's taken a while for this new mind-set to take root and in places the struggle still continues. And when people are placed in specialist facilities (and there can be good reasons for doing so), it should be on a short-term basis but staff there will have to work all the harder to create and maintain an ordinary life for people when resident there.

People are citizens

We've had a change of mind too about what it means to be 'different'. Old notions meant that those deemed to be disabled had not the same entitlements as so-called normal people. This discrimination perpetuated their dependency and justified their exclusion from society. Throughout the last century, civil rights movements argued for equal rights for women, for coloured persons, for gay people. Their case rested not only on concepts of fairness but also on the unique gifts these groups bring to society. Equal rights strengthened the case for people with disabilities to be treated as citizens first and then, as having special needs. Today the force of law is behind this change of mind but it is so recent, that the full ramifications have still to work through service systems[126]. However the basic premise is simple, that everybody is entitled to the same opportunities.

People do not need to be labelled

This point follows from the previous two; we are moving away from grouping people in terms of labels, particularly those that highlight deficits. Nonetheless a rationale remains for doing this; it makes it easier to select who can avail of additional services and supports that can be in short supply. In this respect, the labels are an administrative convenience that can result in benefits for the individual, but often at a cost. The alternative mind-set is a focus on the needs of individuals and we argue that these are met more cost-effectively by tailoring our supports to each person. The range of supports that can be drawn on include high cost specialist services. But relatively few people require such supports for prolonged periods. In future years, new funding arrangements may consolidate a needs-based approach which is already well rooted in educational provision.

A CHANGE OF SPIRIT

By spirit we mean the 'driving force' that fuels your work as a supporter. It's hard to put this notion into words and yet the reality is all too apparent when you compare the way different supporters set about their work. Thankfully many suitable people have been attracted to this work in the past but in the changing job market of the future, we cannot presume that this will continue to happen. We need to be less tolerant of supporters who want to do things their own way and promote instead the need for a particular spirit to inspire their efforts.

More than a job

Throughout we have stressed the importance of mutual relationships but this dimension is rarely mentioned in job descriptions. It cannot be taken for granted. We have identified the personal qualities that are required and these need to be highlighted in the selection of staff, with less emphasis on qualifications for example. We need to nurture these qualities among the existing workforce and recognise those who excel in tangible ways. We need to find leaders who will inspire and guide others in these new styles of working. They are already among us but we may not have seen their full potential.

Finding soul mates

We need to seek out soul mates from among those with whom we work; not in any cliquish way but rather as a source of support for ourselves especially during times of change and we're not quite sure of what to do for the best. They are people we can confide in, whose advice we can trust and who can challenge us. Seeking soul mates recognises that we cannot go it alone, nor should we be expected to, but the search may take some time.

A long-term commitment

Modern society is sold on instant solutions and quick fixes. But there is no magical formula for making people's lives richer and more fulfilled. It requires a long-term commitment as families know when rearing children, or as young people realise when embarking on a career. Throughout there has to be some sense of continuity which can come from the dedication of the same supporters over many years or from the planned replacement of key persons. The high turn-over rates among front-line service staff in parts of the country is especially worrying and needs to be reduced.

We should be able to offer vulnerable people some guarantees of future support which many family carers feel is slipping away with the changes of recent years. Often this reflects their isolation from the management of services and a lack of trust in the people making the decisions. Rekindling a spirit of dedication and commitment is an essential beginning and again, it starts with 'I' not 'them'.

DILEMMAS TO BE FACED

We believe that everything we have written in this book is possible. But we would be less than honest if we didn't admit that our vision creates certain dilemmas; all of which are outside the direct control and influence of most individual supporters to resolve and for which we have no easy answers. But naming them is a step towards their resolution. Services have faced other dilemmas in the past that faded as a consensus grew on new courses of action. We all have to engage in these debates otherwise the dilemmas remain. Here are some topical ones.

Spending priorities

There isn't enough money to do all that needs doing and that will always be true. The case for increased spending has to be constantly made and supported by evidence. But it's also about how money gets spent. For example, an essential debate that needs to occur is the low salaries paid to front-line support workers for the role expected of them. Yet paying people more, often leads to a reduction in the number of available posts, whilst in fact probably more are needed. Are there other cost savings within services that could fund increased salaries for support workers?

Regulation through standardised procedures

People's well-being needs to be safeguarded and services have to account for how they operate. But we wonder if the present approach through regulation and adherence to specified procedures is not ultimately counter-productive for the people being supported in terms of limiting their opportunities. Can we find more flexible and creative ways of monitoring and responding to risk so that their opportunities are widened rather than foreclosed?

Training staff

No one can argue against having a better trained workforce but we can question the topics that are presently given priority and the people invited to act as trainers. Training is a powerful way of conveying the values and priorities of the organisation. For example, is more attention paid to health and safety issues compared to helping new support staff to converse with and listen to the people they support? How involved are those receiving support in the training of paid supporters[127]?

Breakdown of community

A weakening of a sense of community may make it more difficult to recruit people to act as informal supporters. Should our response be to retreat from engaging with the community or should we try to find new ways of engagement that are in tune with modern lifestyles and responsive to local people's availability and needs? For instance, look at the way charities have changed their approach to fund-raising by offering personal challenges of trekking in the Sahara or cycling in the Andes. Would adventure holidays attract people to become involved as supporters and find the sense of belonging to a community that they may well be seeking?

Mainstream or special services

The last century saw an extraordinary growth in specialist supports and services. These brought great gains but they had their shortcomings, notably the social exclusion of the people placed in such services. With this history, it is not easy to gain their access to mainstream services, where the staff feel ill-prepared to work with a clientele who is new and strange to them. They argue too that they are not paid to provide services for this group of people because all the funding is given to specialist services. Addressing these claims will mean devoting more training resources to mainstream personnel and re-aligning the funding that is given to specialist service providers. This is nothing new. A similar re-distribution occurred when institutions closed although at the outset there was great resistance to taking money away from the long-stay hospitals. Perhaps history has to repeat itself?

FEARS FOR THE FUTURE

Nor should we be complacent that advances in human rights will be maintained in future decades. Societies' treatment of people perceived as different is as old as history itself, but in the last two centuries there have been marked swings in societal attitudes. This period begins and ends in optimism. In the early eighteen hundreds the 'moral treatment' movement held sway, based on benevolent psychosocial care and providing guidance in the activities of daily living. In the mid nineteen hundreds the normalisation movement began and evolved into socially inclusive and the person-centred services we see developing today.

But in between was a century and a half of segregation and horrific institutional conditions. This was intensified by the eugenics movement and found its most terrible expression in the concentration camps of Europe where many thousands of people with a disability were murdered. It was feared that 'weak people' would contaminate their country's ambition to move towards ever greater physical, intellectual and societal perfection.

But even at the best of times there has always been an ambivalence lying at the heart of society's thinking about those needing support[128]. Governments were willing to fund moral treatment in the belief that it would teach people with a disability to become productive members of society, a primary value in the Industrial Age. As it became obvious that many would never achieve this goal, there was increasing reluctance to fund such programmes, regardless of the other benefits. They were instead segregated into what began as asylums, or colonies of refuge, but became total institutions. Some of those once most committed to moral treatment ultimately were amongst people's gravest oppressors.[129]

There was likewise considerable ambivalence regarding normalisation. For example in 1982 a prominent psychiatrist published a paper[130] dismissing the humanising efforts of the previous 15 years, including and especially normalisation, as a terrible mistake based on exaggeration and 'anti-intellectualism' and calling for a return to the institutional treatment of the 'intra-psychic' problems of handicapped people, whose need was demonstrated by their alleged failure to function in the community. About the same time, a fellow of the American Association of Mental Deficiency expressed the view that "education and training efforts for the handicapped persons have generally been unsuccessful, and that in any event we should be spending our money on gifted children, who will be the future leaders of our country."[131]

Ambivalence means that societies can swing between a positive and negative view of those needing support, between valuing and supporting people and devaluing them as deviant and unacceptable. It is important to understand that the treatment of 'deviance' in society is based not on scientific or medical advancements, but on the prevailing social and political philosophies. The professional groundwork for the modern era of service provision was laid in the 50s, with the pharmacological breakthroughs and the successes of learning theory: but it was the civil rights movement of the sixties and a U.S. president with a sister with a disability, that generated greater public interest and funding for the closing of institutions along with the emergence of the Normalisation movement into the English speaking world from its roots in the social democracies of Scandinavia.

It is by its very nature that humanity struggles with such ambivalence about those on its margins. We know ourselves to be limited finite beings, vulnerable in the face of life that may overwhelm us and death that certainly awaits us. At the same time we have a sense of ourselves that demands an existence and identity beyond this fear of living and finality of death. This dualism generates great anxiety and is why we strive for social position, power, and possessions as reassuring statements of our self-worth. People who point to human frailty and finiteness, can unconsciously be seen as a threat, particularly at times of upheaval. Many citizens still do not know how to include people needing support into their understanding of society.

The world today faces a major economic, social and political crisis that looks set to continue for some years. As unemployment grows and living standards fall, there is the danger that those at the margins of society may lose out in major ways and that the resources that enable them to know a reasonable quality of life will be greatly diminished.

There is also the possibility that a prolonged economic recession could give rise to powerful social and political movements in which vulnerable people are again placed at risk. The Great Depression, together with the outcomes from World War I, were root causes of the rise of fascism in Europe. People looked to strong, totalitarian leaders to tell them that they were great rather than diminished, and to take them out of their powerlessness and into a new age of supremacy. That 'new age' was one of terror and death for those at the margins of the ideal society who did not conform to the desired image. Such an outcome was a terrible extreme that hopefully will never again arise. But all supporters need to be vigilant in their personal and political lives, for the interests of those they support.

Into the Future

Going into the future with a primary focus on mutual relationships and shared community will not only bring fulfilment to the lives of people needing support (and to their supporters), it will also help to safeguard them in difficult times. The more people are known and cared about in their own communities, the more difficult it will be for those in power to downgrade their needs and rights.

> In this time when we are aiming to become more and more professionalized, we tend to forget that the basis of life is mutual confidence, mutual respect, deep love and acceptance. Once we have this, people can begin to grow.... Often they cannot find people who will live with them – and that does not necessarily mean to occupy the same house. It means to be open, to understand, to share, not to impose but to grow together, in free expression and in liberty, in positive love.[132]

Then the whole of society will gain. Segregation of needy individuals is both a cause and symptom of the dilution or absence of a psychological sense of community.[133] If, instead, we listen to those who need support, our society will be a gentler and more caring place in which all of us can find fulfilment.

One person at a time

And should you feel that all this talk of society and politics is too daunting, we end by reminding you of a theme that has echoed throughout all these pages. Would it make a difference, if instead of trying to solve all the problems of everyone needing support we focussed on just one person at a time?

The starfish story is a lesson for all of us. Of course there are tens of thousands of people who are affected by disabilities and we are often impatient with the pace of change. However making life better for just one person has to be the starting point. As our confidence and influence as supporters grows, other people will also benefit.

The Star-fish story

One day a woman was walking along the sea-shore. She noticed that during the night thousands of starfish had washed up on the shore and they would surely die in the heat of the sun. She came upon a young boy who was methodically picking up a starfish and throwing it backing into the surf. She said to him: "There are thousands of starfish here – how can you possibly expect to make a difference – let nature take its course". The young boy reached down; picked up another star fish and sped it into the sea. Smiling, he turned to the woman and said: "I made a difference for that one!"

Maybe it is not a case of getting the big picture sorted out first, but rather like a jig-saw, it's constructing the big picture from its individual elements, one step at a time. That's a task in which we all have a part to play, whoever we are and wherever we live.

NOTES

[1] American Psychologist, Special Edition, 2000.
[2] Scottish Executive (2000b); Department of Health (2001); DHSSPS (NI) (2005)
[3] O'Brien (1989)
[4] Swain & French (2000)
[5] Wolfensberger (1988)
[6] Dykens (2005)
[7] Mullins (1987)
[8] Hornby (1994); Mardell (2005)
[9] Hastings and Taunt (2002)
[10] Glidden & Johnson (1999)
[11] Hastings et al (2002)
[12] Connors and Stalker (2002)
[13] Hastings and Horne (2004)
[14] Vanier and Kearney (1981)
[15] Rhodes (1975)
[16] Walsh (1997)
[17] Pueschel (1990)
[18] Emerson et al (2005); Curtice (2006); O'Brien et al (2009); Association for Self-Advocacy: Croatia et al (2007)
[19] Reinders (2002)
[20] Wolfensberger (1972)
[21] Atkinson & Williams (1990)
[22] Oliver (1996)
[23] Goode (1998)
[24] Edgerton (1993)
[25] Mansell and Ericcson (1994)
[26] Holm, Holst, Balch Olsen, and Perlt, (1996)
[27] Ward (1998)
[28] Emerson et al (2005); Curtice (2006); O'Brien et al (2009); Association for Self-Advocacy: Croatia et al (2007)
[29] Schalock et al (2002)
[30] De Walle et al (2005)
[31] Emerson (2001)
[32] Algozzine (2001)
[33] Department of Health and Home Office (2000)
[34] Canadian Association of Rehabilitation Professionals (2002)
[35] Schon (1987)
[36] Clapton & Kendall (2002)
[37] Department of Health and Home Office (2000)
[38] Ward (1998); Lawton (2006)
[39] http://www.valuingpeople.gov.uk/dynamic/valuingpeople136.jsp
[40] Scottish Executive (2000a)
[41] Argyle (1988)
[42] Collier (2000)
[43] Dennis (1995)
[44] Purcell, McConkey & Morris, I. (2000)
[45] McConkey, R., Purcell, M. & Morris, I. (1999)
[46] Schaufeli & Enzmann (1998)

47   Skinner (2005)
48   Morrison (2005)
49   Flannery 2001
50   Rogers (1961)
51   Pringle (1986)
52   Duck (1991)
53   Blatt & Kaplan (1966)
54   Vanier (1999)
55   Oswin (2000)
56   Hollins et al (2003)
57   Firth & Rapley (1990)
58   Schwartz (1992)
59   Edgerton (1993)
60   http://www.disabilitynow.org.uk/timetotalksex/index.htm
61   Simons (1998)
62   Information Plus (2006)
63   Walsh (1986)
64   Simpson et al (2006)
65   McCarthy (1999)
66   Britsh Institute of Learning Disabilities (BILD) (2000)
67   http://www.fpa.org.uk/Shop/Learningdisabilitiespublications/Allaboutus
68   Fanstone & Katrak (2003)
69   McCarthy & Thompson (1994)
70   McVilly et al (2006)
71   Emerson et al (2005)
72   Robertson et al (2005)
73   McMillan, D. & Chavis, D. (1986)
74   Dunne, J. (1986)
75   Hearne and Dunne (1992)
76   www.sharedcarenetwork.org.uk
77   Bayley (1997)
78   Emerson and McVilly (2004)
79   http://circlesnetwork.org.uk; Neville et al (1995)
80   Mansell et al (2005)
81   Baron and Haldane (1992)
82   Vanier (1989).
83   Vanier (1989)
84   Lawler (1998)
85   http://www.camphill.org.uk/
86   McConkey et al (2007)
87   Collins and McConkey (2007)
88   McConkey (1994)
89   Scottish Consortium for Learning Disability (2006)
90   Triangle Housing Association (2008)
91   Brown (2009)
92   Leach (2002)
93   Beyer et al (1996)
94   Bradley (1999)
95   Brown (2009)
96   Goodley and Moore (2002)
97   Collins and McConkey (2007)
98   http://www.newhorizonspartnership.co.uk

[99] Woodcock and Narayan (2000); Bates and Davis (2004)
[100] Cameron and Quinn (1999)
[101] Payne (2000)
[102] Greenleaf (1998)
[103] Council on Quality and Leadership (2005)
[104] Foster-Turner (2005)
[105] Morrison (2005)
[106] Greco and Sloper (2004)
[107] Scottish Consortium for Learning Disability (2006)
[108] Nolan (1987)
[109] Sellars (2002)
[110] Pountney (2007)
[111] Power (2004)
[112] O'Brien, O'Brien, Schwartz (2004)
[113] Kinsella (2000)
[114] Hickson and Khemka (1999)
[115] e.g. Adults with incapacity (Scotland) Act (2000)
[116] De Walle et al (2005)
[117] Murphy and O'Callaghan (2004)
[118] Swinton (2001)
[119] Hatton et al. (2004)
[120] Hatton et al (2004)
[121] Fry (2000)
[122] Harrington (2000)
[123] Mosteller (1981)
[124] Hatton et al. (2004)
[125] Brooke (2001)
[126] Hughes and Coombs (2001)
[127] Jones and Robertson (2007)
[128] Mittler (1979)
[129] Wolfensberger (1969); Ryan and Thomas (1980)
[130] Goldberg (1982)
[131] Quoted by Haywood, C. (1981).
[132] Vanier, J. (1975)
[133] Sarason (1974)

REFERENCES

Abbott, S., & McConkey, R. (2006). The barriers to social inclusion as perceived by people with intellectual disabilities. *Journal of Intellectual Disabilities, 10*, 275–287.

Algozzine, B., Browder, D., Karvonen, M., Test, D. W., & Wood, W. M. (2001). Effects of interventions to promote self-determination for individuals with disabilities. *Review of Educational Research, 71*(2), 219–277.

American Psychologist. (2000). *Positive psychology: An introduction* (M. E. P. Seligman & M. Csikszentmihalyi, Eds.).

Argyle, M. (1988). *Bodily communication*. London: Routledge.

Association for Self Advocacy, Croatia, Association for Promoting Inclusion, Croatia & Inclusion Europe. (2007). *Human rights of persons with intellectual disability: Country report Croatia*. Brussels: Inclusion Europe.

Atkinson, D., & Williams, F. (1990). *Know me as I am: An anthology of prose, poetry and art by people with learning disabilities*. London: Hodder & Stoughton in association with Open University.

Baron, S. R., & Haldane, J. D. (1992). *Community normality and difference. Meeting special needs*. Aberdeen: Aberdeen University Press.

Bates, P., & Davis, F. A. (2004). Social capital, social inclusion and services for people with learning disabilities. *Disability and Society, 19*(3), 195–207.

Bayley, M. (1997). *What price friendship: Encouraging the relationships of people with learning difficulties*. Wootton Courtenay: Hexagon Publishing.

Berscheid, E., & Peplau, L. A. (1983). The emerging science of relationships. In H. Kelly, et al. (Eds.), *Close relationships*. San Francisco: Freeman.

Beyer, S., Goodere, L., & Kilsby, M. (1996). *Costs and benefits of supported employment agencies: Findings from a national survey. Employment Service Research Series R37*. London: Stationery Office.

Blatt, B., & Kaplan, F. (1966). *Christmas in purgatory*. Boston: Allyn & Bacon.

Bradley, A. (1999). *Taking turns: Around leisure and recreation*. Kidderminster: BILD Publications.

British Institute of Learning Disabilities. (2000). *Social and personal relationships: Policy and good practice guidelines for staff working with adults with learning disabilities*. Kidderminster: BILD.

Brooke, B. (2001). Faith and Light. In B. Kelly & P. McGinley (Eds.), *Intellectual disabilities: The response of the church*. Chorley, Lancashire: Lisieux Hall Publications.

Brown, R. (2009). Adult education and intellectual and allied developmental disabilities. In *International Encyclopaedia of Rehabilitation*. Retrieved from http://cirrie.buffalo.edu/encyclopedia/article.php?id=21&language=en

Cameron, K. S., & Quinn, R. E. (1999). *Diagnosing and changing organizational culture*. Reading, MA: Addison Wesley.

Canadian Association of Rehabilitation Professionals. (2002). *Canadian code of ethics for rehabilitation professionals*. Toronto: CARP Inc.

Clapton, J., & Kendall, E. (2002). Autonomy and participation in rehabilitation: Time for a new paradigm? *Disability and Rehabilitation, 24*, 987–991.

Collier, B. M. (2000). *See what we say: Situational vocabulary for adults who use augmentative and alternative communication*. Baltimore: Paul H. Brookes.

Collins, S., & McConkey, R. (2007). *At home in the community? Promoting the social inclusion of people with a learning disability living in supported accommodation*. Ballymoney: Triangle Housing Association and University of Ulster.

Connors, C., & Stalker, K. (2002). *The views and experiences of disabled children and their siblings: A positive outlook*. London: Jessica Kingsley Publishers.

Council on Quality and Leadership. (2005). *Quality measures 2005*. Towson, MA: Council.

Curtice, L. (2006). *How is it going? A survey of what matters to people with learning disabilities in Scotland today*. Glasgow: Enable.

REFERENCES

Dennis, J. (1995). *Hearing problems in people with Down Syndrome: Notes for parents and carers.* London: Down's Syndrome Association. Retrieved from http://www.downs-syndrome.org.uk/pdfs/dsa-medical-series-4.pdf

Department of Health. (2001). *Valuing people: A new strategy for the 21st century.* London: Department of Health.

Department of Health and Home Office. (2000). *No secrets: Guidance on developing and implementing multi-agency policies and procedures to protect vulnerable adults from abuse.* London: DoH.

DHSSPS (NI). (2005). *Equal lives: Review of policy and services for people with a learning disability in Northern Ireland.* Belfast: Department of Health, Social Services and Public Safety.

De Walle, I., van Loon, J., van Hove, G., & Schalock, R. L. (2005). Quality of life vs. quality of care: Implications for people and programs. *Journal of Policy and Practice in Intellectual Disabilities, 2,* 229–239.

Duck, S. (1991). *Understanding relationships.* New York: Guilford Press.

Dunne, J. (1986). Sense of community in l'Arche and in the writings of Jean Vanier. *Journal of Community Psychology, 14,* 6–23.

Dykens, E. M. (2005). Happiness, well-being, and character strengths: Outcomes for families and siblings of persons with mental retardation. *Mental Retardation, 43,* 360–364.

Edgerton, R. B. (1993). *The cloak of competence: Stigma in the lives of the mentally retarded* (Rev. and updated ed.). Berkley, CA: University of California Press.

Emerson, E. (2001). *Challenging behaviour: Analysis and intervention in people with severe intellectual disabilities.* Cambridge: Cambridge University Press.

Emerson. E., & McVilly, K. (2004). Friendship activities of adults with intellectual disabilities in supported accommodation in Northern England. *Journal of Applied Research in Intellectual Disabilities, 17,* 191–197.

Emerson, E., Malam, S., Davies, I., & Spencer, K. (2005). *Adults with learning difficulties in England 2003/04.* London: NHS Health and Social Care Information Centre.

Fanstone, C., & Katrak, Z. (2003). *Sexuality and learning disability: A resource for staff.* London: Family Planning Association.

Firth, H., & Rapley, M. (1990). *From acquaintance to friendship: Issues for people with learning disabilities.* Worcester: British Institute of Mental Handicap.

Flannery, R. B. (2001). The Assaulted Staff Action Program (ASAP): Ten year empirical support for Critical Incident Stress Management (CISM). *International Journal of Emergency Mental Health, 3,* 5–10.

Foster-Turner, J. (2005). *Coaching and mentoring in health and social care: The essential manual for professionals and organisations.* Oxford: Radcliffe Publishing.

Fry, P. S. (2000). Religious involvement, spirituality and personal meaning for life: Existential predictors of psychological wellbeing in community-residing and institutional care elders. *Aging & Mental Health, 4,* 375–387.

Glidden, L. M., & Johnson, V. E. (1999). Twelve years later: Adjustment in families who adopted children with developmental disabilities, *Mental Retardation, 37,* 16–24.

Goldberg, G. (1982). *Anti-psychiatric and anti-professionalism.* Paper presented at IASSMD conference, Toronto.

Goode, B. (1998). cited in Ward (1998).

Goodley, D., & Moore, M. (2002). *Disability arts against exclusion: People with learning difficulties and their performing arts.* Kidderminster: BILD.

Greco, V., & Sloper, P. (2004). Care co-ordination and key worker schemes for disabled children: Results of a UK-wide survey. *Child: Care, Health & Development, 30,* 13–20.

Greenleaf, R. K. (1998). *The power of servant leadership.* San Francisco: Berrett-Koehler.

Harrington, S. (2000). Affectivity and symbol in the process of catechesis. In B. Kelly & P. McGinley (Eds.), *Intellectual disabilities: The response of the church.* Chorley, Lancashire: Lisieux Hall Publications.

Hastings, R. P., Allen, R., McDermott, K., & Still, D. (2002). Factors related to positive perceptions in mothers of children with intellectual disabilities. *Journal of Applied Research in Intellectual Disabilities, 15*, 269–275.

Hastings, R. P., & Horne, S. (2004). Positive perceptions held by support staff in community mental retardation services. *American Journal on Mental Retardation, 109*, 53–62.

Hastings. R. P., & Taunt, H. (2002). Positive perceptions in families of children with developmental disabilities. *American Journal on Mental Retardation, 107*, 116–127.

Hatton, C., Turner, S., Shah, R., Rahim, N., & Stansfield, J. (2004). *Religious expression: A fundamental human right*. London: Foundation for People with a Learning Disability.

Haywood, C. (1981). Presidential Address to the American Association of Mental Deficiency.

Hearne, M., & Dunne, J. (1992). *Home sharing: An evaluation of family based respite care*. Galway: Galway County Association.

Hickson, L., & Khemka, I. (1999). Decision making and mental retardation. In L. M. Glidden (Ed.), *International review of research in mental retardation* (Vol. 22). San Diego: Academic Press.

Hollins, S., Dowling, S., & Blackman, N. (2003). *When somebody dies*. London: Gaskell & St. George's Medical School.

Holm, P., Holst, J., Balch Olsen, S., & Perlt, B. (1996). Quality of everyday life: The Danish approach. In J. Tossebro, A. Gustavsson, & G. Dyrendahl (Eds.), *Intellectual disabilities in the Nordic welfare states. Policies and everyday life*. Kristiansand: Norwegian Academic Press.

Hornby, G. (1994). *Disability counselling: Professionals and parents working together*. Cheltenham: Nelson Thornes.

Hughes, A., & Coombs, P. (2001). *Easy guide to the Human Rights Act 1998*. Kidderminster: BILD.

Information Plus. (2006). *Lifeball special: An interactive approach to social skills for adults with learning disabilities*. Brighton: Pavilion Publishing.

Interaction Institute for Social Change. (2000). *Building successful partnerships*. Cambridge, MA: Interaction Institute.

Jones, J., & Robertson, C. (2007). *Partnerships for training: An easy access pack for developing equal training partnerships with people with a learning disability*. Kidderminster: BILD.

Kinsella, P. (2000). Person-centred risk assessment. Retrieved from http://valuingpeople.gov.uk/dynamic/valuingpeople141.jsp

Lawler, G. (1998). Accommodating difference – The Camphill approach to meeting special needs. *Irish Journal of Social Work Research, 1*, 29–42.

Lawton, A. (2006). *A voice of their own: A toolbox of ideas and information for non-instructed advocacy*. Kidderminster: BILD.

Leach, S. (2002). *A supported employment workbook using individual profiling and job matching*. London: Jessica Kingsley Publishers.

McCarthy, M. (1999). *Sexuality and women with learning disabilities*. London: Jessica Kingsley Publishers.

McCarthy, M., & Thompson, D. (1994). *Sex and staff training – A training manual for staff working with people with learning difficulties*. Brighton: Pavilion Publishing.

McConkey, R. (1994). *Innovations in educating communities about learning disabilities*. Chorley: Lisieux Hall Publications.

McConkey, R., Abbott, S., Noonan-Walsh, P., Linehan, C., & Emerson, E. (2007). Variations in the social inclusion of people with intellectual disabilities in supported living schemes and residential settings. *Journal of Intellectual Disability Research, 51*(3), 207–217.

McConkey, R., Purcell, M., & Morris, I. (1999). Staff perceptions of communications with a partner who is intellectually disabled. *Journal of Applied Research in Learning Disabilities, 12*, 204–210.

McMillan, D., & Chavis, D. (1986). Sense of community: A definition and theory. *Journal of Community Psychology, 14*, 6–23.

McVilly, K. R., Stancliffe, R. J., Parmenter, T. R., & Burton-Smith, R. M. (2006). 'I get by with a little help from my friends': Adults with intellectual disability discuss loneliness. *Journal of Applied Research in Intellectual Disabilities, 19*, 191–203.

REFERENCES

Mansell, J., Beadle-Brown, J., Ashman, B., & Ockenden, J. (2005). *Person-centred active support: A multi-media training resource for staff to enable participation, inclusion and choice for people with learning disabilities.* Brighton: Pavilion Publishing.

Mansell, J., & Ericcson, K. (1994). *The dissolution of institutions: An international perspective.* London: Chapman & Hall.

Mardell, D. (2005). *Danny's Challenge: Learning to love my son.* London: Short Books.

Mittler, P. (1979). *People not patients: Problems and policies in mental handicap.* London: Routledge.

Morrison, T. (2005). *Staff supervision in social care: Making a real difference for staff and service users.* Brighton: Pavilion Publishing.

Mosteller, S. (1981). Living with. In *The challenge of l'Arche.* Minneapolis, MN: Winston Press.

Mullins, J. B. (1987). Authentic voices from parents of exceptional children. *Family Relations, 36,* 30–33.

Murphy, G. H., & O'Callaghan, A. (2004). Capacity of adults with intellectual disabilities to consent to sexual relationships. *Psychological Medicine, 34,* 1347–1357.

Neville, M., et al. (1995). *Circles of support: Building inclusive communities.* Rugby: Circles Network.

Nolan, C. (1987). *Under the eye of the clock.* London: Pan Books.

O'Brien, J. (1989). *What's worth working for? Leadership for better quality human services.* Syracuse: Responsive Systems Associates.

O'Brien, J., O'Brien, C. L., & Schwartz, D. B. (2004). *What can we count on to make and keep people safe? Perspectives on creating effective safeguards for people with developmental disabilities.* Syracuse: Responsive Systems Associates.

O'Brien, P., McConkey, R., Curry, P., Wolfe, M., & Roberts, W. (2009). *All we want to say: A national survey of people with intellectual disabilities.* Dublin: National Institute for Intellectual Disability, Trinity College.

Oliver, M. (1996). *Understanding disability: From theory to practice.* Basingstoke: Macmillan.

Oswin, M. (2000). *Am I allowed to cry?* (2nd ed.). London: Souvenir Press.

Payne, M. (2000). *Teamwork in multiprofessional care.* Chicago: Lyceum Books.

Pountney, J. (2007). *Protecting people who have a learning disability from abuse.* Kidderminster: BILD.

Power, M. (2004). *The risk management of everything. Rethinking the politics of uncertainty.* London: Demos.

Pringle, M. L. K. (1986). *The needs of children.* London: Routledge.

Pueschel. (1990). Clinical aspects of Down syndrome from infancy to adulthood. *American Journal of Medical Genetics,* Suppl. 7, 52–56.

Purcell, M., McConkey, R., & Morris, I. (2000). Staff communication with people with intellectual disabilities: the impact of a work-based training programme. *International Journal of Language and Communication Disorders, 35,* 147–158.

Reinders, J. S. (2002). The good life for citizens with intellectual disability. *Journal of Intellectual Disability Research, 46,* 1–5.

Rhodes, W. (1975). *Behavioral threat and community response: A community psychology inquiry.* New York: Behavioral Books.

Robertson, J., Emerson, E., Hatton, C., Elliot, J., et al. (2005). The impact of person-centred planning. Lancaster University: Institute of Health Education.

Rogers, C. (1961). *On becoming a person: A therapist's view of psychotherapy.* London: Constable.

Ryan, J., & Thomas, F. (1987). *The politics of mental handicap* (Rev. ed.). London: Free Association Books.

Sarason, S. (1974). *The psychological sense of community: Prospects for community psychology.* San Francisco: Jossey-Bass.

Schalock, R. L., Brown, I., Brown, R., Cummins, R. A., Felce, D., Matikka, L., et al. (2002). Conceptualization, measurement, and application of quality of life for persons with intellectual disabilities: Report on an international panel of experts. *Mental Retardation, 40,* 457–470.

Schaufeli, W., & Enzmann, D. (1998). *The burnout companion to study and practice: A critical analysis.* London: Taylor & Francis.

Schon, D. A. (1987). *Educating the reflective practitioner: Toward a new design for teaching and learning in the professions.* San Fransciso: Jossey-Bass.

Schwartz, D. B. (1992). *Crossing the river: Creating a conceptual revolution in community and disability.* Cambrdge, MA: Brookline Books.

Scottish Consortium for Learning Disability. (2006). *Making connections: Stories of local area co-ordination in Scotland.* Glasgow: Scottish Consortium. Retrieved from http://uk.geocities.com/localareacoordination/

Scottish Executive. (2000a). *Independent advocacy: A guide for commissioners.* Edinburgh: HMSO.

Scottish Executive. (2000b). *The same as you? A review of services for people with learning disabilities.* Edinburgh: HMSO.

Sellars, C. (2002). *Risk assessment in people with learning disabilities.* London: BPS Blackwell.

Simons, K. (1998). *Living support networks: An evaluation of the services provided by KeyRing.* Brighton: Pavilion Publishing.

Simpson, A., Lafferty, A., & McConkey, R. (2006). *Out of the shadows: A report of the sexual health and wellbeing of people with learning disabilities in Northern Ireland.* London: Family planning Association.

Skinner, K. (2005). *Continuing professional development for the social services workforce in Scotland.* Dundee: Scottish Institute for Excellence in Social Work Education.

Swain, J., & French, S. (2000). Towards an affirmation model of disability. *Disability & Society, 15,* 569–582.

Swinton, J. (2001). *A space to listen: Meeting the spiritual needs of people with a learning disability.* London: The Mental Health Foundation.

Swinton, J. (2002). Spirituality and the lives of people with learning disabilities and review. *Tizard Learning Disability Review, 7,* 29–35.

Triangle Housing Association. (2008). *Social inclusion for people with learning disabilities: CD Rom Toolkit.* Ballymoney: Triangle Housing.

Vanier, J. (1975). *Be not afraid.* New York: Paulist Press.

Vanier, J. (1989). *Community and growth* (Rev. ed.). New Jersey, NJ: Paulist Press.

Vanier, J. (1999). *Becoming human.* New Jersey, NJ: Paulist Press.

Vanier, J., & Kearney, T. (1981). The prophetic cry: Interview with Jean Vanier. *Crane Bag, 5,* 79–85.

Walsh, J. (1986). *Let's make friends.* London: Souvenir Press.

Walsh, P. N. (1997). Old World-new territory: European perspectives on intellectual disability. *Journal of Intellectual Disability Research, 41,* 112–118.

Ward. L. (1998). *Innovations in advocacy and empowerment for people with intellectual disabilities.* Chorley: Lisieux Hall Publications.

Wolfensberger, W. (1969). The origin and nature of our institutional models. In R. B. Kugel, et al. (Eds.), *Changing patterns in residential services for the mentally retarded.* Washington DC: The President's Committee on Mental Retardation.

Wolfensberger, W. (1972). *The principle of normalisation in human services.* Toronto: The National Institute of Mental Retardation.

Wolfensberger, W. (1988). Common assets of mentally retarded people that are commonly not acknowledged. *Mental Retardation, 26,* 63–70.

Woolcock, M., & Narayan, D. (2000). Social capital: Implications for developmental theory, research and policy. *World Bank Research Observer, 15,* 225–249.

Breinigsville, PA USA
28 February 2010
233296BV00003B/15/P